PAPERBACK SONGS

MOTOWN HITS

MELODY LINE, CHORDS AND LYRICS
FOR KEYBOARD • GUITAR • VOCAL

HAL•LEONARD®

ISBN 0-7935-9823-0

Visit Hal Leonard Online at
www.halleonard.com

Welcome to the PAPERBACK SONGS SERIES.

Do you play piano, guitar, electronic keyboard, sing or play any instrument for that matter? If so, this handy "pocket tune" book is for you.

The concise, one-line music notation consists of:

MELODY, LYRICS & CHORD SYMBOLS

Whether strumming the chords on guitar, "faking" an arrangement on piano/keyboard or singing the lyrics, these fake book style arrangements can be enjoyed at any experience level – hobbyist to professional.

The musical skills necessary to successfully use this book are minimal. If you play guitar and need some help with chords, a basic chord chart is included at the back of the book.

While playing and singing is the first thing that comes to mind when using this book, it can also serve as a compact, comprehensive reference guide.

However you choose to use this PAPERBACK SONGS SERIES book, by all means have fun!

CONTENTS

(contents continued)

ABC

Words and Music by ALPHONSO MIZELL,
FREDERICK PERREN, DEKE RICHARDS and BERRY GORDY

With drive
G C
You went to school to learn, girl, things you
Read - ing and writ - ing, 'rith - me - tic are the
G C
nev - er, nev - er knew be - fore, like
branch - es of the learn - ing tree. With -
G C
"I" be - fore "E" ex - cept af - ter "C" and why
out the roots of a love ev - 'ry day girl, your
G C G Cmaj7
two plus two makes four. Now, now, now, I'm gon - na teach you all
ed - u - ca - tion ain't com plete. Teach - er's gon - na show you how
Gmaj7 C G C
a - bout love, dear. Sit your - self down; take a seat;
to get an "A". Spell me you add the two,
G C
all you got - ta do is re - peat af - ter me:
lis - ten to me ba - by, that's all you got - ta do.

G
Cmaj7
G
Cmaj7
A B C eas - y as 1 2 3 as sim-ple as
G
C
G
C
Do, Re, Mi; A ___ B C; 1 2 3; ba-by, you and me girl;
G
Cmaj7
G
Cmaj7
A B C eas - y as 1 2 3 as sim-ple as
G
C
Do, Re, Mi; A ___ B C;
G
C
1
1 2 3; ba - by, you and me girl.
G
C
Come on, let me love you just a lit - tle bit;
G
C
G
I'm gon - na teach you how to sing it out;

C
Cmaj7
2
Com-a, com-a, come on let me show you what it's all a-bout.
Yah
3
sit down girl
I think I love you
No get up girl
show me what you can do.
G
C
3
Shake it, shake it ba - by come on now
G
C
shake it, shake it ba - by, Oo,
G
C
D.S. and Fade
Shake it, shake it ba - by hey.

AIN'T NO MOUNTAIN HIGH ENOUGH

Words and Music by NICKOLAS ASHFORD
and VALERIE SIMPSON

Bm
Gmaj7
Em9
F♯m7
e - nough, ain't no val - ley low
Bm
Gmaj7
Em9
F♯m7
e - nough, ain't no riv - er wide
Bm
Esus
E
D/F♯
G
e - nough to keep me from get - ting to you,
1
babe. Re - mem - ber the day
2
A7sus
babe. And no wind, and no rain
A/G
F♯sus
F♯
or win - ter's cold
B7sus
B7
Gmaj7
can stop me, ba - by. Oh, ba -

A/G
- by if you are my
(If you're
Bm/A A Bm/A A Bm/A
goal.
ev - er in trou - ble, I'll be there on the dou - ble. Just
Cm/B♭ B♭ Fm E♭/G Fm7♭5/C♭
send for me ba - by! Oh, ba - by!)
Cm7/B♭ Am7♭5
My love is a - live deep down in my heart,
A♭maj7 Gm7 Fm9 E♭/G A♭ F7/A
al - though we are miles a - part. If you ev - er
Cm7/B♭ Am7♭5
need a help - ing hand, I'll be there on the dou -
A♭maj7 Gm7 Fm7 Gm7
ble just as fast as I can. Don't you know that there

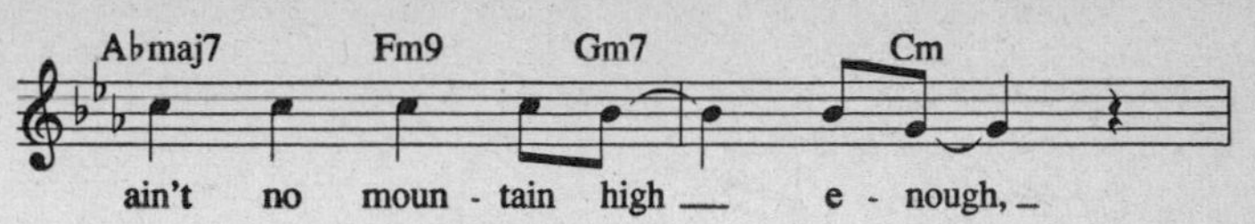
A♭maj7 Fm9 Gm7 Cm
ain't no moun - tain high e - nough,

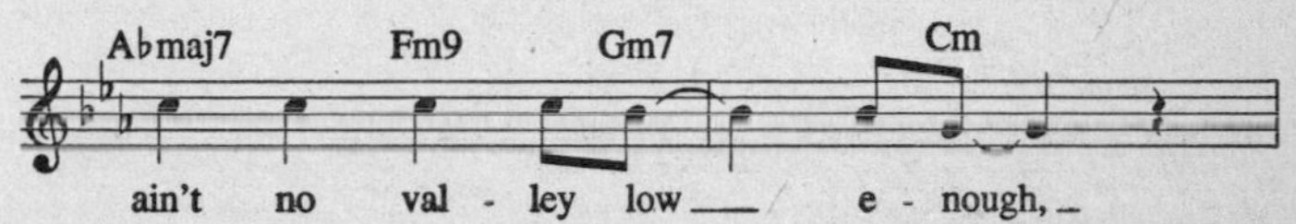
A♭maj7 Fm9 Gm7 Cm
ain't no val - ley low e - nough,

A♭maj7 Fm9 Gm7 Cm
ain't no riv - er wide e - nough to

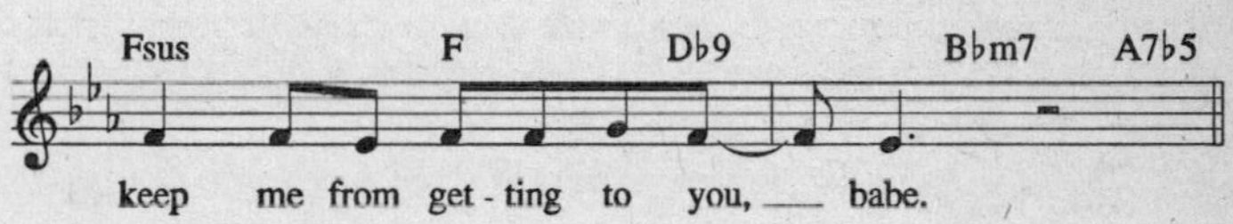
Fsus F D♭9 B♭m7 A7♭5
keep me from get - ting to you, babe.

A♭maj7 N.C.
Ain't no moun - tain high e - nough,

Gm7 N.C.
ain't no val - ley low e - nough,

Fm9 N.C.
ain't no riv - er wide e - nough to

1
E♭maj7 Gm7/C C7

keep me from you.

2
E♭maj7 Gm7/C C7

keep me from you.

A♭m7/D♭ G♭maj7

(Instrumental)

A♭m7/D♭ B♭m7 E♭9sus E♭7

A♭m7/D♭ G♭maj7

Ah.

A♭m7/D♭ G♭maj7 E♭9sus E♭7

Noth-ing can keep me, keep me from you.

A♭m7/D♭ G♭maj7

Ain't no moun-tain high e-nough.

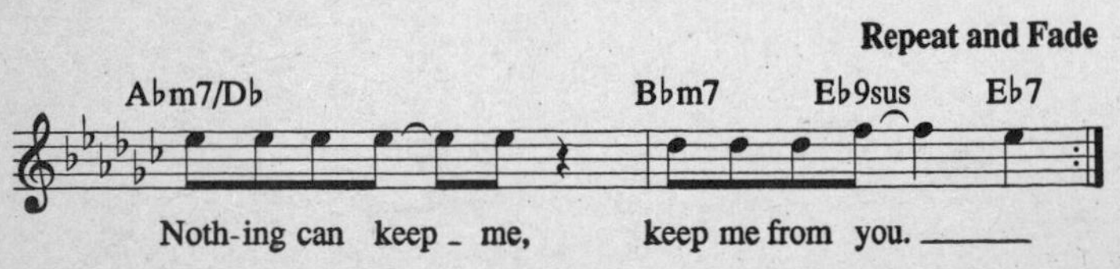

BABY LOVE

Words and Music by BRIAN HOLLAND, EDWARD HOLLAND and LAMONT DOZIER

F Bb Am
I do wrong to make you stay a -
like you do, I guess it's me
love with you. ba - by, ba - by
To Coda
Gm7 C7 F
way so long 'cause Ba - by Love, my
ooh, need to hold you once a -
ooh, 'til it
F7 D7
Ba - by Love, been miss - ing ya, miss
gain my love, feel your warm em -
Gm Bb6
kiss - ing ya. In - stead of
brace my love. Don't throw our
F
break - ing up,
love a - way,
Bb6 F
let's start some kiss - ing and mak - ing up.
please don't do me this way.

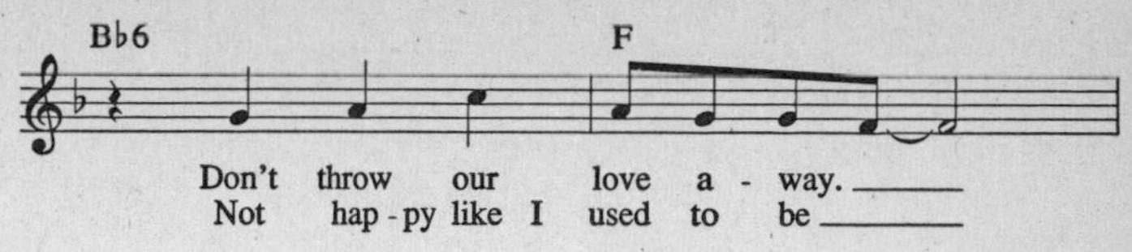
B♭6
F
Don't throw our love a - way.
Not hap - py like I used to be

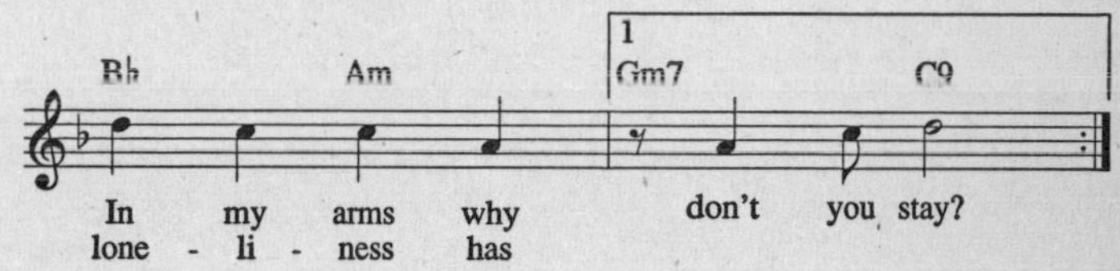
1
B♭
Am
Gm7
C9
In my arms why don't you stay?
lone - li - ness has

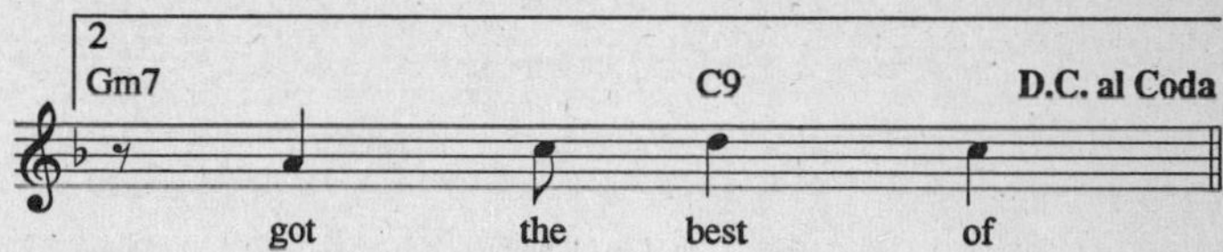
2
Gm7
C9
D.C. al Coda
got the best of

CODA
F
F7
hurt me, 'til it hurt me.

D7
Gm
Ooh
Ba - by Love,

B♭6
F
Repeat and Fade
Don't throw our love a - way.

AIN'T NOTHING LIKE THE REAL THING

Words and Music by NICKOLAS ASHFORD
and VALERIE SIMPSON

A♭maj7 G
it can't see or come to me __ when I
Cm7 B♭m E♭7 A♭ E♭/G
call your name. _ I re - al - ize _ it's just a pic - ture
E♭
in a frame. ________ I read your
E♭ Fm E♭/G
let - ters when you're not near, ______ but
mem - 'ries to look back on. ______
A♭maj7 G
they don't move _ me and they don't groove _ me like
Though they help __ me when you phone, _ I'm
Cm7
when I hear ______ your _
well a - ware ______ noth -
B♭m7 E♭7 A♭ E♭/G
__ sweet voice ______ whis - per - ing ________
- ing can ______ take the place of your

Eb
in my ear. Don't you know,
be - ing there.
Ebmaj7
Ain't noth - ing like the
So glad we got the
Fm/Eb Eb Fm/Eb Eb Abmaj7
To Coda
real thing, ba - by. Ain't noth - ing like the
real thing, ba - by. So glad we got the
Fm7 Fm7/Bb Eb Fm Eb/G
real thing. I play my game, a fan - ta - sy.
Abmaj7 G Cm7
I pre-tend, but I know in re - al - i - ty I
Bb7 Eb7 Ab
need the shel - ter of your arms to
Eb
com - fort me. No oth - er

Gm7 G7
sound is quite the same as your
Cm E♭7/B♭ E♭7
name. No touch can do half as
A♭ E♭/B♭
much to make me feel
C♯dim Fm7
bet - ter. So, let's stay to -
Fm7/B♭ D.S. al Coda
geth - er. I've got some
CODA
Fm7 Fm7/B♭
real thing.
E♭ E♭maj7 Fm/E♭ E♭ Fm/E♭ E♭
Ain't noth - ing like the real thing, ba - by.
Repeat and Fade
A♭maj7 Fm7 Fm7/B♭
Ain't noth - ing like the real thing.

AIN'T TOO PROUD TO BEG

Words and Music by EDWARD HOLLAND
and NORMAN WHITFIELD

Moderately, with a beat
G
C
1. I know _ you wan - na leave me, but I re -
2.-4. See additional lyrics
G
C
fuse to let you go. If I have to
G
C
beg, plead _ for your sym - pa - thy, I don't mind
G
D11
'cause you mean that much to me. Ain't too proud to
G
C
G
C
beg and you know it. Please don't leave
G
C
G
C
me, girl, don't you go. Ain't too proud to

G
C
G
C
plead, ___ ba - by, ba - by. Please don't leave_

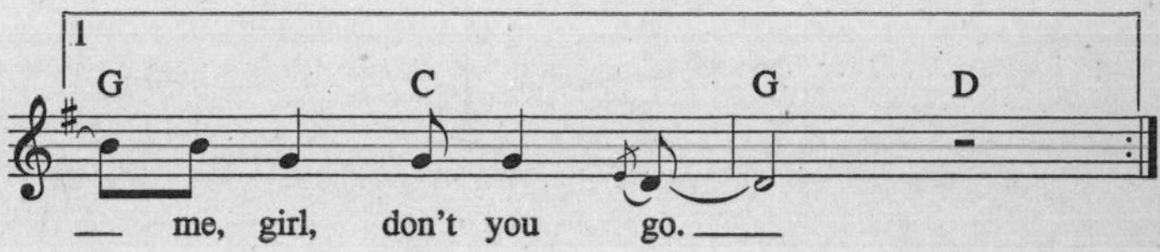
1
G
C
G
D
___ me, girl, don't you go. ___

2
G
C
G
___ me, girl, don't you go. ___

Additional Lyrics

2. Now I've heard a cryin' man
Is half a man with no sense of pride,
But if I have to cry to keep you,
I don't mind weepin' if it'll keep you by my side.
Chorus

3. If I have to sleep on your doorstep all night and day
Just to keep you from walking away,
Let your friends laugh, even this I can stand,
'Cause I wanna keep you any way I can,
Chorus

4. Now I've got a love so deep in the pit of my heart,
And each day it grows more and more,
I'm not ashamed to call and plead to you, baby,
If pleading keeps you from walking out that door.
Chorus

BACK IN MY ARMS AGAIN

Words and Music by BRIAN HOLLAND,
LAMONT DOZIER and EDWARD HOLLAND

Moderately
C
1. All day long I hear my tel - e - phone ring, friends
2. ea - sy for friends to say let him go, but
3. See additional lyrics
call - ing giv - ing their ad - vice.
I'm the one who needs him so.
F/C C
From the boy I love I should
It's his love that
break a - way 'cause heart-aches he'll bring one day.
makes me strong; with - out him I can't go on.
F/C C F
I lost him once through
This time I'll live my

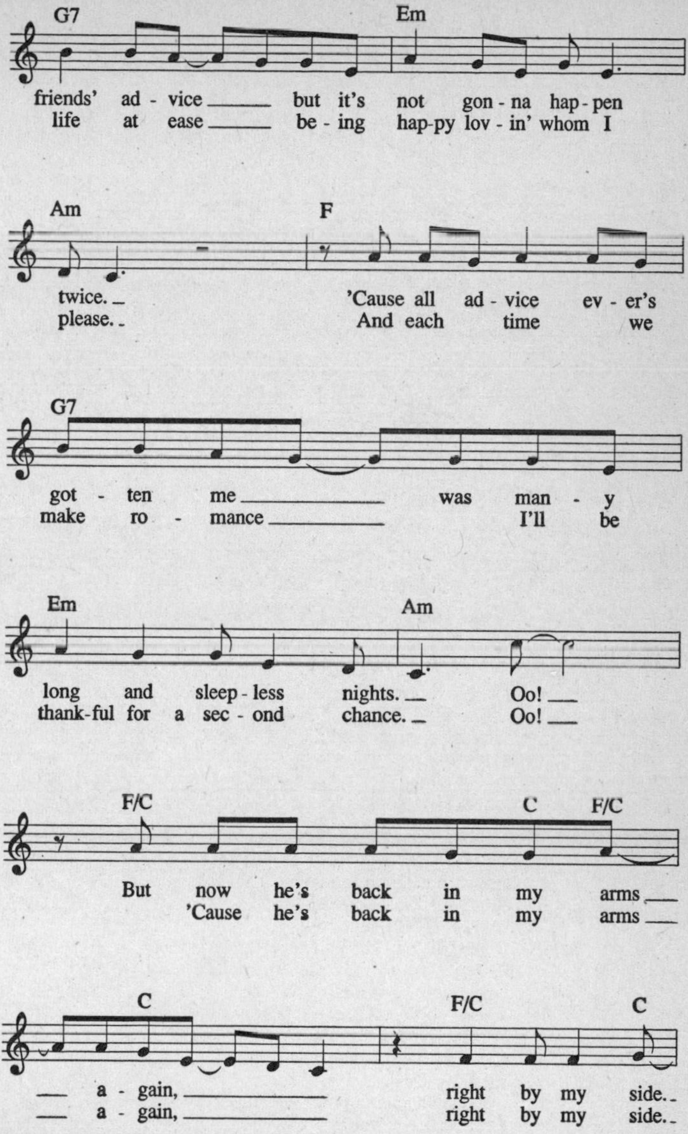

G7 Em
friends' ad - vice ___ but it's not gon - na hap - pen
life at ease ___ be - ing hap-py lov - in' whom I

Am F
twice. _ 'Cause all ad - vice ev - er's
please. _ And each time we

G7
got - ten me ___ was man - y
make ro - mance ___ I'll be

Em Am
long and sleep - less nights. ___ Oo! ___
thank-ful for a sec - ond chance. _ Oo! ___

F/C C F/C
But now he's back in my arms ___
'Cause he's back in my arms ___

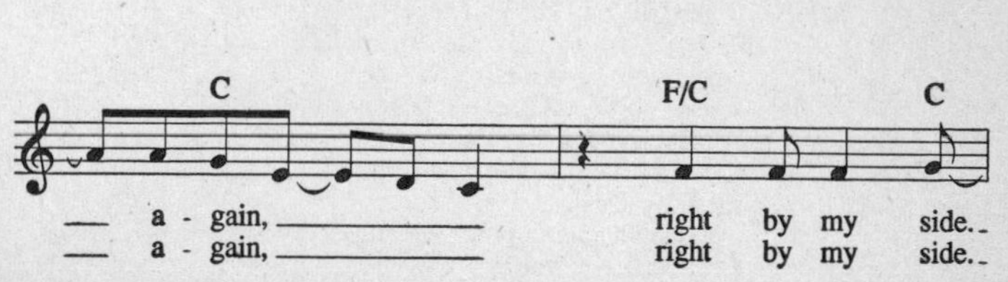
C F/C C
___ a - gain, ___ right by my side. _
___ a - gain, ___ right by my side. _

F/C
C F/C
I got him back in my arms
I've got him back in my arms
C
a - gain,
a - gain,
1
F/C
C
so sat - is - fied
oo. It's
2,3
F/C
C
D.C. for 3rd Verse
so sat - is - fied
oo.
C F/C
C
Repeat and Fade
I'm sat - is - fied.
so sat - is - fied.
Yeah,

Additional Lyrics

3. How can Mary tell me what to do
When she lost her love so true;
And Flo, she don't know
'Cause the boy she loves is a Romeo.
I listened once to my friend's advice
But it's not gonna happen twice.
'Cause all the advice ever's gotten me
Was many long and sleepless nights. Oo!
I got him back in my arms again.
Right by my side.
I got him back in my arms again
So satisfied. *(Fade)*

BEN

Words by DON BLACK
Music by WALTER SCHARF

Moderately
F
Ben, the two of us need
Ben, you're al - ways run - ning
C7/E
F
look no more, we both found what we were
here and there, you feel you're not want - ed
C7/E
F
look - ing for. With a friend to call my
an - y - where. If you ev - er look be -
A7sus
A7/C#
own, I'll nev - er be a -
hind and don't like what you
Eb9#11
D7
lone, and you my friend will
find there's some - thing you should
Gm7b5/Db
C7
see, you've got a friend in
know you've got a place to

1
F Bb/F F Bb/F
me.
2
F Bb F Bb
go. I
Gm C7/E Fmaj7 F6
used to say I and me,
Gm C7/E F
now it's us, now it's we. I
Gm C7/E Fmaj7 F6
used to say I and me,
Gm C7/E F
now it's us, now it's we.
Ben, most peo - ple would turn

C7/E
F
you a - way, I don't lis - ten to a
C7/E
F
word they say. They don't see you as I
C7/E
do, I wish they would try
E♭7
D7
to I'm sure they'd think a -
Gm7♭5/D♭
C7
F
Gm7/F
gain if they had a friend like Ben. Chorus: (Like
F
Gm7/F
F
Gm7/F
Ben) Like Ben, (Like
F
Gm7/F
F
Ben) Like Ben.

BERNADETTE

Words and Music by BRIAN HOLLAND,
LAMONT DOZIER and EDWARD HOLLAND

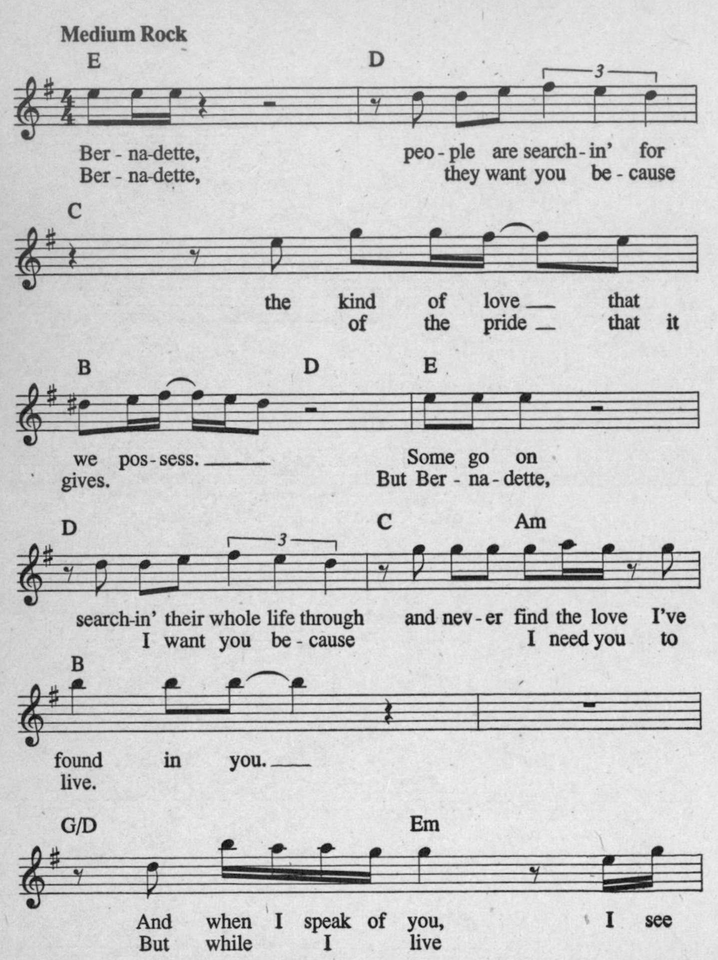

Am7
Am7/D
en - vy in oth - er men's ___ eyes.
on - ly to ___ hold ___ you.
G/D
Em
Am7
Am7/D
And I'm well a - ware_ of what's on their minds.
Some ___ oth - er men_ they long to con - trol you.
Am7
G/B
They pre - tend to be my friend _ when
But ___ how can they con - trol ___ you,
Am7/D
D7
Am7
G/B
all the time they long to _ per-suade you from_
Ber - na-dette, when they can - not con - trol them-selves,
Am7/D
D7
1
Am7
G/B
___ my side. They'd give the world_ and all_ they own for
Ber-na-dette, from
Am7/D
D7
just one mo - ment we have known._
2
Am7
Bm
Am7/D
D7
want - ing you, need - ing you, but dar - ling, you be-long ___

E
D
to me.
I'll tell the world
you be-long
C
to me.
I'll
B
D
tell the world
you're the soul of
E
D
me.
I'll tell the world
you're a part of
C
Am
B
me.
Ber - na-dette.
G
In
your arms I
C
Em
find the kind of peace of mind
the world is search-ing
B
G
for.
But you.
you give me the
3

C
Em
joy this heart of mine has al - ways been long - ing
B
G/D
Em
for. In you I have what
Am7
Am7/D
oth - er men long for.
G/D
Em
Am7
Am7/D
All men need some-one to wor - ship and a-dore.
Am7
G/B
That's why I treas - ure you and
Am7/D
D7
place you high a - bove.
Am7
G/B
Am7
D7
For the on-ly joy in life is to be loved.
Am7
Bm
So what - ev - er you do,

Am7/D
D7
Ber - na - dette,
keep on
E
D
lov - ing me.
Ber - na - dette,
keep on
C
B
need - ing me.
Ber - na - dette.
N.C.
E
Ber-na-dette.
Ber-na-dette,
you're the
Ber-na-dette,
you mean
D
soul of me,
more than a
more to me
than a wom -
Repeat and Fade
C
B
D
dream.
You're a prayer to me.
an
was ever meant to be.

DANCING IN THE STREET

Words and Music by MARVIN GAYE,
IVY HUNTER and WILLIAM STEVENSON

New Or - leans, _ up in New York Cit -
___ now, _ and if we get to Mo-tor Cit-
y. All ___ we need ___ is mu -
y. All ___ we need ___ is mu -
A7
- sic, sweet mu - sic. ___ There'll be
- sic, sweet mu - sic. ___ There'll be
mu - sic ev - 'ry - where. _
mu - sic ev - 'ry - where. _
There'll be
E7
swing - ing, ______ sway - ing, and
To Coda
rec - ords play - ing and
danc - ing ___ in the street. ___ Oh, ________

G#
— it does-n't mat - ter — what you wear — just as
C#m7
long as you are — there. — So come on, — ev -
F#7
- 'ry guy — grab a girl. —
A
Ev - 'ry - where — a - round —
A/B
— the world — they'll be — E7
danc - ing. —
They're danc - ing in the — street. —
D.S. al Coda
— Oo. This is an

CODA
dancing in the street. Yeah.
E7
(Instrumental)
1-3
4
G#
Ah. Oh, it doesn't matter
C#m
what you wear just as long as you are there.
So come on, ev-
F#7
'ry guy grasp a girl.

A7
Ev - 'ry - where a - round
A/B
the world
Amaj7/B
they'll be
E7
danc - ing.
They're danc-ing in the street.
Phil - a - del - phia P. A.,
Balt - i-more and D. C. now,
And if we get to that Mo - tor Cit - y,
Ah,
way down in L. A., Cal-i - for-ni-a.
Repeat and Fade

CLOUD NINE

Words and Music by BARRETT STRONG
and NORMAN WHITFIELD

Moderately, with double time feeling

D7#9

Child - hood part of my life, it was - n't ver - y

pret - ty. You see, I was

born and raised ___ in the slums of the

cit - y. It was a

one room shack that slept ten oth - er chil - dren be -

sides me. ___ We hard - ly had e-nough food or room to

sleep. It was hard ___ times,

need - ed some-thing to ease my trou - bled
D
mind.
Lis - ten!
My
D7
fa-ther did-n't know the mean-ing of
work,
he
dis - re-spect-ed ma-ma, and treat-ed us like dirt.
I
left home, seek - in' a job that I nev - er did
find,
de -
pressed and down-heart - ed I took to
D
D7#9
Cloud Nine I'm do - in' fine,

— up here on Cloud Nine. Lis - ten
one more time, — I'm do - in' fine, —
— up here on Cloud Nine.
Folks down there tell me, they say,
G
"Give your-self a chance son, don't let life pass you by." But the
D7
world of re - al - i - ty is a rat race where
G
3
3
on - ly the strong - est sur - vive. It's a
D
3
dog eat dog world, and that ain't no

G7
lie. Lis - ten! It ain't
A7
e - ven safe no more to
walk the streets at night, I'm do - in'
D7#9
D
fine ___ on Cloud
D7
Nine. Let me tell you a - bout Cloud Nine. _ Cloud
3
D7
Nine, you can be what you wan - na be (Cloud
Nine) You ain't got no re -
spon - si - bi - li - ty, and ev - 'ry man, _ ev - 'ry

man is free (Cloud Nine) and you're a mil - lion miles

1

from re - al - i - ty.

I wan - na say I

D7#9 G

love the life I live, ___ and I'm gon - na

D7

live the life ___ I ___

G D

love up here on Cloud Nine. _

— on Cloud Nine, you're as free as a
bird in flight, (Cloud Nine) there's no dif-f'rence be-tween
day and night. (Cloud Nine) It's a world of love
— and har-mo-ny, (Cloud Nine) you're a mil-lion miles
from re - al - i - ty. Cloud
2
D7#9
D7
from re - al - i - ty. (Cloud
Repeat and Fade
Nine)
(Cloud

DEVIL WITH THE BLUE DRESS

Words and Music by WILLIAM STEVENSON
and FREDERICK LONG

Medium Rock
C7
(1., 3.) Fee fee fi fi fo fo fum.
(2.) Wear-in' her per - fume, Cha - nel Num-ber Five,
Look-in' might - y nice, here she comes,
Got to be the fin - est wom - an a - live.
wear-in' a wig, hat and shades to match; got
Walks so smooth catch-es ev - ery-bod - y's eye,
high heel sneak-ers and an al - li - ga - tor hat.
got to be love - ly, you can't say good-bye. She's
F7
Wear-in' her pearls and a dia - mond ring, she got
not too skin-ny and not too fat, she's a
C7
brace-lets on her fin-gers and - a ev - er - y - thing.
real hum - ding - er and I like it like that.

G7
Dev - il with a blue dress, blue dress, blue dress,
F7
dev - il with a blue dress on.
C F/C C F
Dev - il with a blue dress, blue dress, blue dress,
C F C G7sus
dev - il with a blue dress on.
C7
(Instrumental)
To Coda
C Eb F G Bb C Eb F
N.C.
D.C. al Coda
CODA

DO YOU LOVE ME

Words and Music by
BERRY GORDY

Moderate Rock
Eb
Do you love me? I can
Ab Bb Eb
real - ly move. Do you love me? I said I'm
Ab Bb Eb
in the groove. Do you love me? Do
Ab Bb Ab
you real - ly love me now, now that I,
To Coda Bb
I can dance?
Ab/Eb Eb7
Watch me now! Work, work, 1. gon - na
2. See additional lyrics

Db/Eb Ab Ab/Eb Eb
work it out ba - by. Work, work, drive
Db Ab Ab/Eb Eb
me cra - zy. Work, work, with a
Db/Eb Ab Ebsus
lit - tle bit of soul child!
Ab/Eb Eb
(1.,2.) For rock - in' and roll - in',
Db/Eb Ab Ab/Eb Eb
rock - in', roll - in', do the slam.
Db Ab Ab/Eb Eb
do the slam. Tell me ba - by,
Db/Eb Ab
do you like
tell me ba - by;

Ab/Eb
Eb
Db
Ab
it like that? like it like that. Come on and
Bb7
tell me, Yeah, tell
Bb7sus
Bb7
me, yeah, tell me, yeah. yeah.
1st time D.S.
2nd time D.S. al Coda
N.C.
Do you love
CODA
N.C.
(Instrumental)
1-5
6
Db
Ab
Do you love

Additional Lyrics

2. C'mon, wind me up baby,
   Drive me crazy.
   Ah, but you're gettin' kind of cold, child...

DON'T YOU WORRY 'BOUT A THING

Words and Music by
STEVIE WONDER

B+/F
G
But don't you wor - ry 'bout a thing,
But don't you wor - ry 'bout a thing,
Don't you wor - ry 'bout a thing,
G7
Bm
don't you wor - ry 'bout a thing, ma - ma.
don't you wor - ry 'bout a thing, ma - ma.
don't you wor - ry 'bout a thing, pret-ty ma - ma.
Cmaj7
A7
'Cause I'll be stand - in'
on the side
on the side
in the wings
To Coda
C/D
1
Gmaj7
when you check it out.
B+
2
G
G♭
They say out,
F
E
E♭
D
G
G(add9)
when you get

G
G♭
F
E
off
E♭
D
G
G(add9)
your trip.
Don't you wor - ry 'bout a
Em
B+
thing,
Em7
Em6/B
Fmaj7
Em7
B+
don't you wor - ry 'bout a
thing.
Em7
Em6/B
Fmaj7
Em
B+
Ba
bum
ba,
bum
ba

Em7
A7
Dm
G9
bum, ba
bum. Bum bum, bum bum, bum bum.
1
Cmaj7
B+/F
2
Cmaj7
B+/F
Ba
G
Don't you wor - ry 'bout a thing,
G7
Bm
don't you wor - ry 'bout a thing, ma - ma.
Cmaj7
Amaj7
'Cause I'll be stand - ing on the side
C/D
G
G♭
when you check it out,
F
E

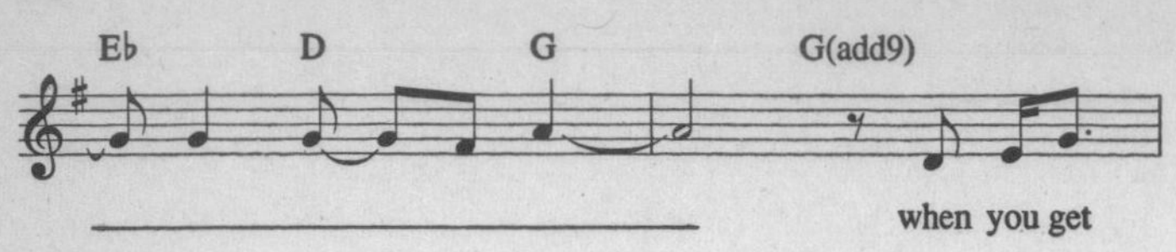
E♭
D
G
G(add9)
when you get

G
G♭
F
E
off

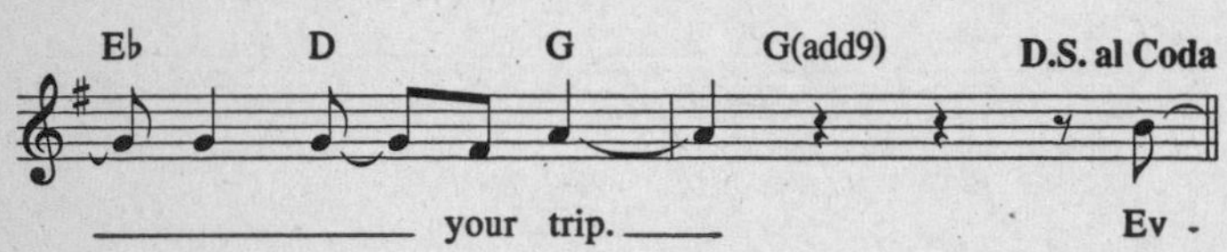
E♭
D
G
G(add9)
D.S. al Coda
your trip.
Ev -

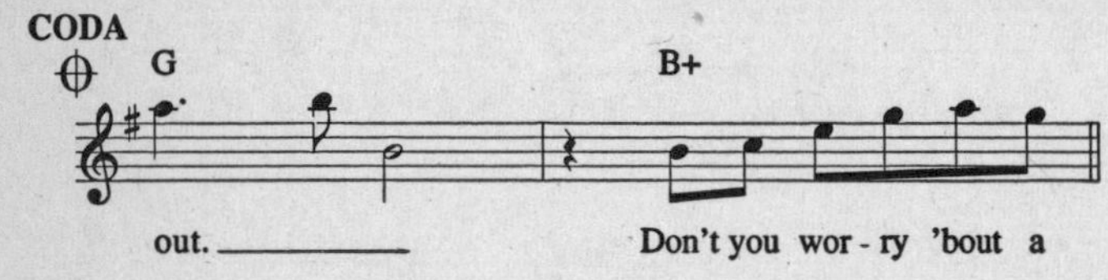
CODA
G
B+
out.
Don't you wor - ry 'bout a

Em
B+
Em7
Em6/B
thing,

Fmaj7
Repeat ad lib. and Fade
don't you wor - ry 'bout a

FOR ONCE IN MY LIFE

Words by RONALD MILLER
Music by ORLANDO MURDEN

B♭ F7/C B♭/D
some - how I know I'll be strong. For
B♭ B♭6 D+
once I can touch what my heart used to dream of
E♭ Cm F7 B♭maj7 Dm
long be - fore I knew some - one warm like
Gm Gm7 C7
you would make my dream come
Cm7 F7 B♭ B♭+
true. For once in my life I won't
B♭6 Bdim7 Cm A♭/C
let sor - row hurt me, not like it's hurt me be -
F7 G7 Cm A♭/C
fore. For once I have some - thing I
F7 F7♯5 B♭ F7/C
know won't de - sert me, I'm not a - lone an - y -

Bb/D
Bb
Bb6
more. For once I can say this is
D+
Eb
mine, you can't take it, long as I know I have
C9/E
1
Bb/F
Bb+
love, I can make it. For once in my life I have
Eb/Bb
Cm7/F
F7
Bb
some - one who needs me.
C9
F7
2
Bb/F
Bb+
For once I can feel that some -
Cm7
F7
F#dim7
Gm
bod - y's heard my plea.
C9
Bb
Bb+
For once in my life I have
Eb/Bb
Cm7/F
F7
Bb
Gb/Bb
Bb6/9
some - one who needs me.

EASY

Words and Music by
LIONEL RICHIE

Moderately
Ab
Cm7
Bbm7
Bbm7/Eb
Know it sound fun-ny, but I just can't stand the pain;
Ab
Cm7
girl, I'm leav - ing you to - mor - row.
Bbm7
Bbm7/Eb
Ab
Cm7
Seems to me, girl, you know I've done all
Bbm7
Bbm7/Eb
Ab
Cm7
I can.
You see, I begged, stole and I bor-
Bbm7
- rowed,
yeah.
Bbm7/Eb
Ab
Cm7
Ooh,
that's why I'm eas - y.
Bbm7
Bbm7/Eb
I'm eas - y like Sun - day morn -

Ab Cm7 Bbm7 Bbm7/Eb
- ing. That's why I'm eas -
Ab Cm7
- y.
Bbm7 Bbm7/Eb
I'm eas - y like Sun - day morn -
To Coda
Gb Db/F Db/Eb Ab
- ing.
Cm7 Bbm7 Bbm7/Eb
Why in the world would an-y-bod-y put chains on me?
Ab Cm7 Bbm7 Bbm7/Eb
3
I've paid my dues to make it.
Ab Cm7
Ev - 'ry - bod - y wants me to be what they want
Bbm7 Bbm7/Eb Ab Cm7
me to be. I'm not hap - py when I try to fake

Bbm7
it,
no.
Bbm7/Eb
D.S. al Coda
Ooh,
that's why I'm eas -
CODA
Ab
Gbmaj7
Fm7
ing
I wan-na be
high,
so
Ebm7 Ebm7/Ab Db/F
Gbmaj7
Fm7
high.
I wan-na be
free to know the things I do are right.
Ebm7
Ebm7/Ab
Db
I wan - na be free,
Gbmaj7
Fm7
just
Ebm7
Ebm7/Ab
me,
oh,
babe.
Cb/Gb
Gb/Db
Cb/Eb
Db
(Instrumental)

Ab
Cm7
Bbm7
Bbm7/Eb
Instrumental solo
Ab
Cm7
1
Bbm7
Bbm7/Eb
2
Bbm7
Ab
Cm7
Solo ends
That's why I'm eas - y.
Bbm7
Bbm7/Eb
I'm eas - y like Sun - day morn -
Ab
Cm7
Bbm7
Bbm7/Eb
- ing.
That's why I'm eas -
Ab
Cm7
- y.
Bbm7
Bbm7/Eb
I'm eas - y like Sun - day morn -
Repeat and Fade
Ab
Cm7
Bbm7
Bbm7/Eb
- ing.
'Cause I'm eas -

HEATWAVE
(Love Is Like a Heatwave)

Words and Music by EDWARD HOLLAND, LAMONT DOZIER and BRIAN HOLLAND

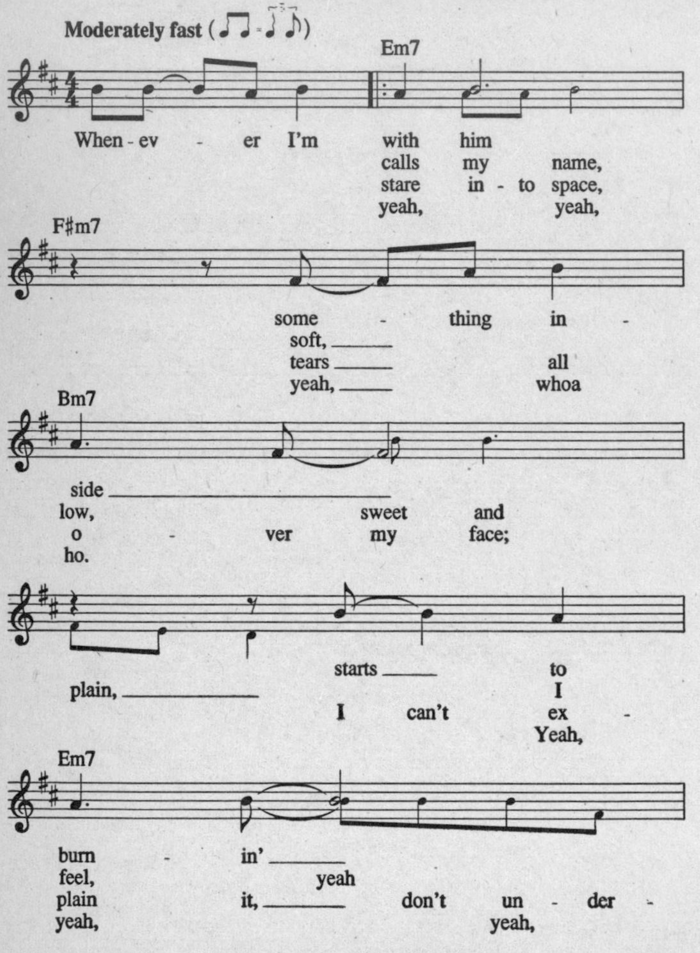

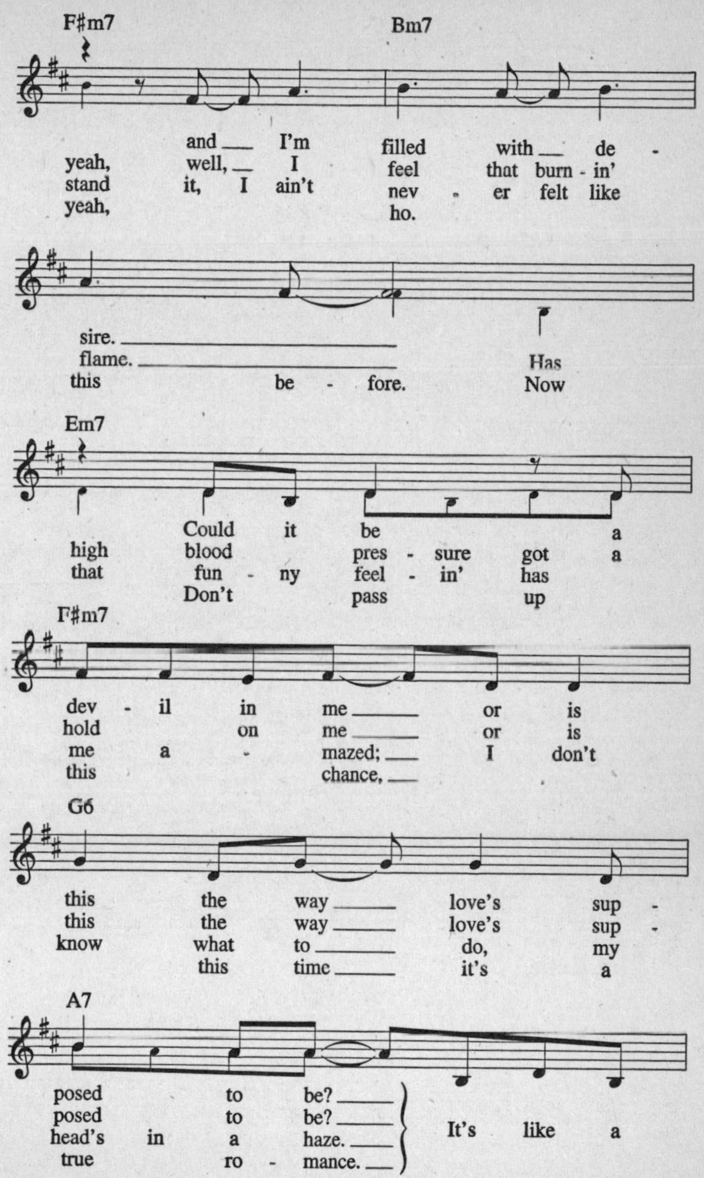
F♯m7
Bm7
and ___ I'm filled with ___ de -
yeah, well, ___ I feel that burn - in'
stand it, I ain't nev - er felt like
yeah, ho.
sire. ___
flame. ___
this be - fore.
Has
Now
Em7
Could it be a
high blood pres - sure got a
that fun - ny feel - in' has
Don't pass up
F♯m7
dev - il in me ___ or is
hold on me ___ or is
me a - mazed; ___ I don't
this chance, ___
G6
this the way ___ love's sup -
this the way ___ love's sup -
know what to ___ do, my
this time ___ it's a
A7
posed to be? ___
posed to be? ___
head's in a haze. ___
true ro - mance. ___
It's like a

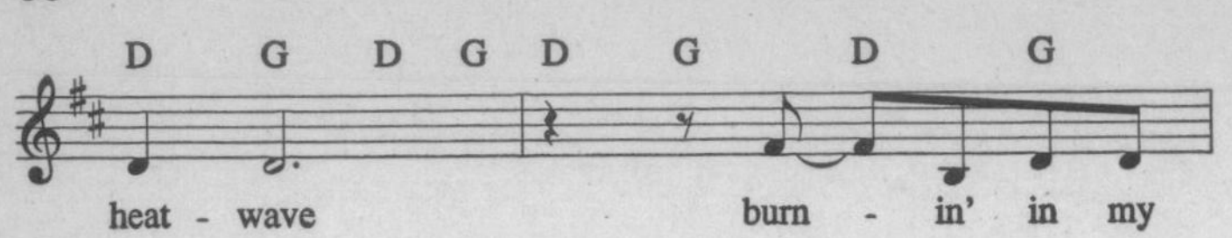
D G D G D G D G
heat - wave burn - in' in my

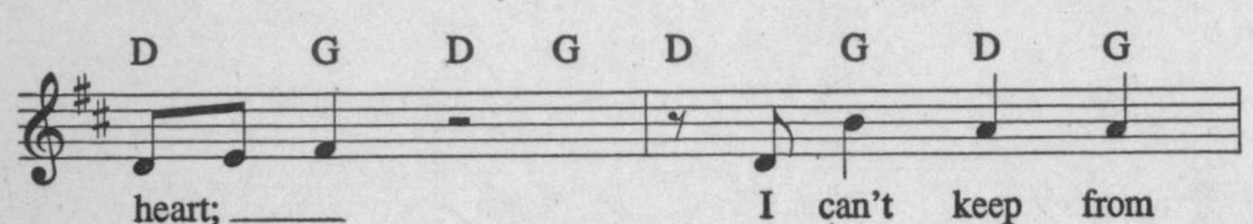
D G D G D G D G
heart; I can't keep from

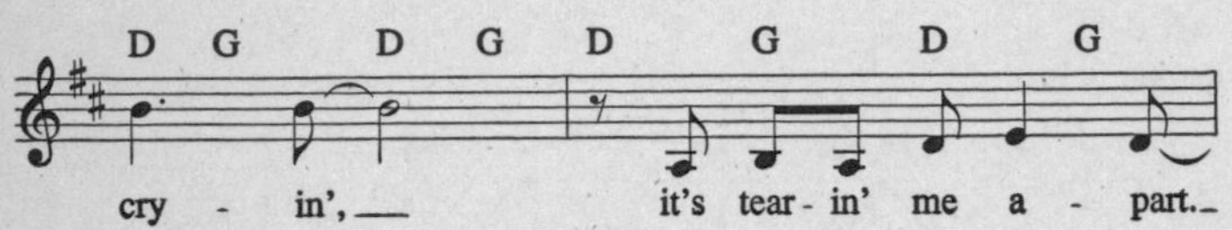
D G D G D G D G
cry - in', it's tear - in' me a - part.

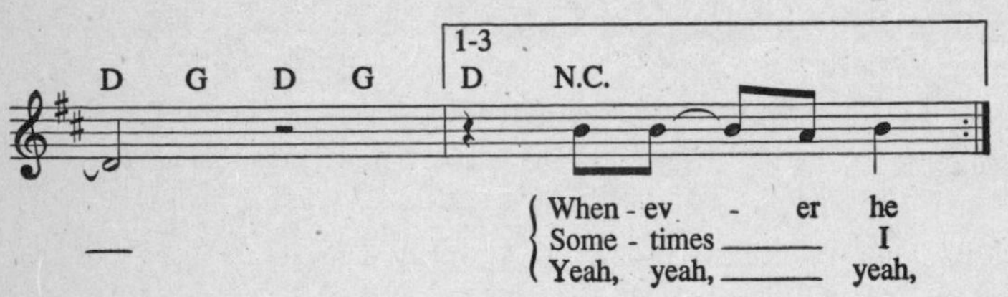
1-3
D G D G D N.C.
When - ev - er he
Some - times I
Yeah, yeah, yeah,

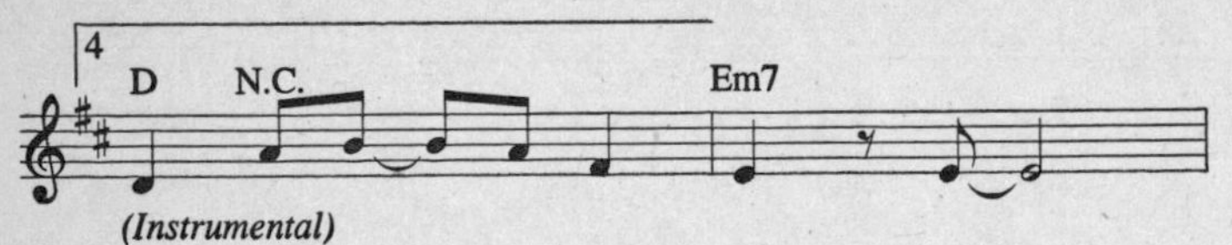
4
D N.C. Em7
(Instrumental)

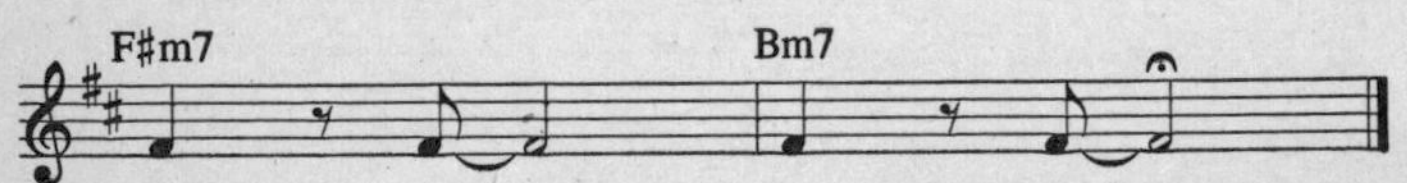
F#m7 Bm7

I HEARD IT THROUGH THE GRAPEVINE

Words and Music by NORMAN J. WHITFIELD
and BARRETT STRONG

Em
A7
found out yes - ter - day. Don't you know that I heard
loved some - one else. In - stead I heard
Em
A7
Em
A
it through the grape - vine, not much long -
it through the grape - vine, not much long -
Em
- er would you be mine. Uh huh,
- er would you be mine. Oh, I heard
A7
Em
heard it through the grape - vine. Oh, I'm just
it through the grape - vine. And I'm just
A7
a - bout to lose my mind.
a - bout to lose my mind.
Em
Hon-ey, hon-ey oh yeah.
(I heard it through the grape-vine, not much
long - er would you be mine, ba -

Additional Lyrics

3. People say believe half of what you see
Oh, and none of what you hear;
But I can't help but be confused
If it's true please tell me dear.
Do you plan to let me go
For the other guy you loved before?

HEAVEN HELP US ALL

Words and Music by
RONALD MILLER

Db
Ab
turns his back a - way. Heav-en help the man who kicks the
Db
Eb7
Db
man who has to crawl. Heav - en help us
Ab
Bbm7
Ab7
Db
all; Heav - en help us all;
Eb7
Ab
Bbm7 Ab7
Db
Heav - en help us all,
Eb7
Ab
Bbm Ab
Bbm
help us all. Heav-en help us, Lord
C7
Fm
Fm7
hear our call when we call.
Bb7
Eb7
E7
Oh yeah,
A
A7
Heav - en help the boy yeah, who

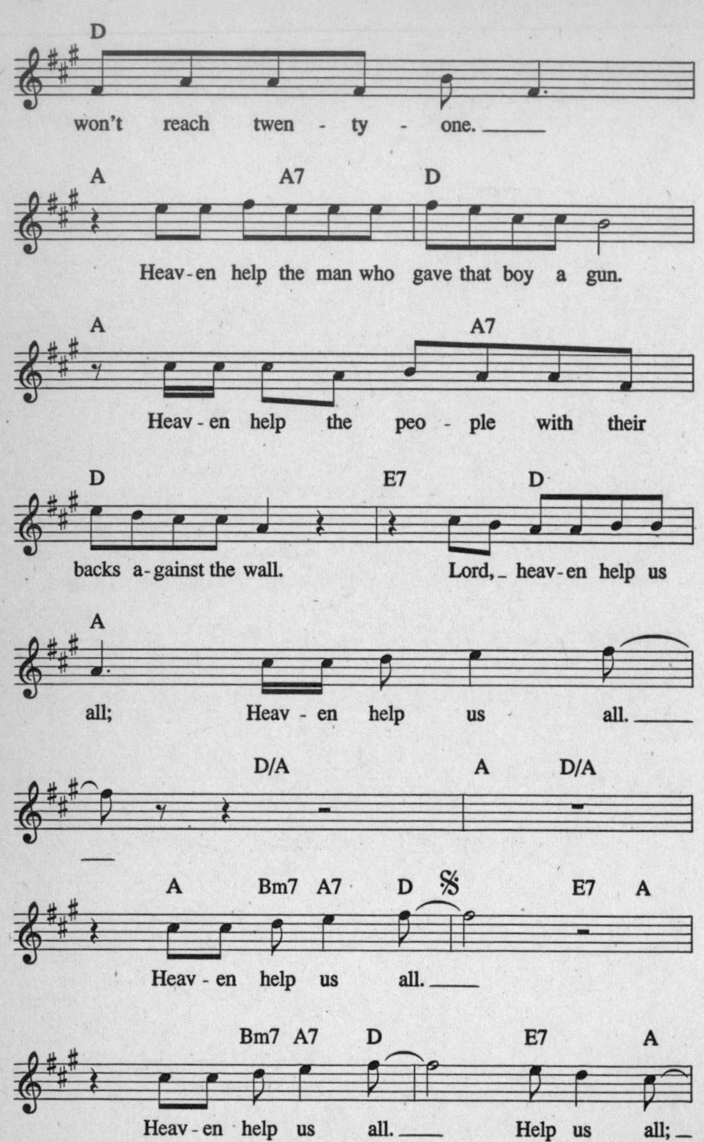
D
won't reach twen - ty - one.
A A7 D
Heav-en help the man who gave that boy a gun.
A A7
Heav - en help the peo - ple with their
D E7 D
backs a-gainst the wall. Lord, heav-en help us
A
all; Heav - en help us all.
D/A A D/A
A Bm7 A7 D E7 A
Heav - en help us all.
Bm7 A7 D E7 A
Heav - en help us all. Help us all;

Bm A Bm
heav - en help us; Lord,
C#7 F#m F#m7
Hear our call. When we call
B7 E7
help us
A D/A A D/A A
all.
(Spoken:) Now I lay me
D/A A D/A
down before I go to sleep in a troubled world, I pray the Lord to keep, keep
A D/A E7 D
hatred from the mighty and the mighty from the small. Heaven help us
A
all
3
Oh, oh, oh, yeah
D.S. and Fade
Bm7 A7 D
Heav - en help us all.

I CAN'T GET NEXT TO YOU

Words and Music by BARRET STRONG
and NORMAN WHITFIELD

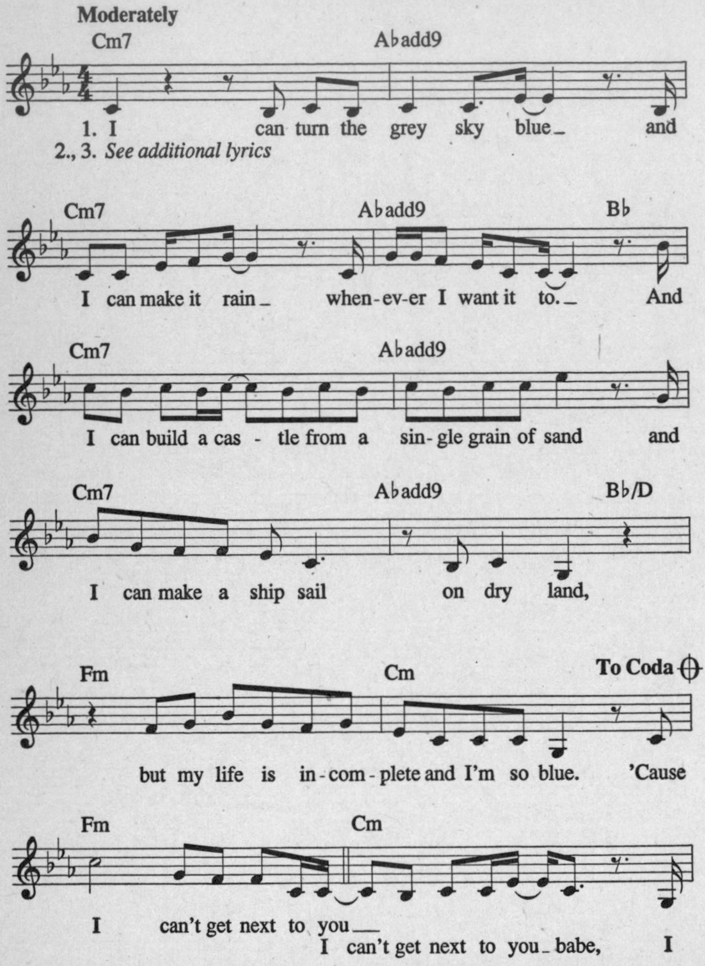

Moderately

Cm7 Ab add9

1. I can turn the grey sky blue_ and
2., 3. *See additional lyrics*

Cm7 Ab add9 Bb

I can make it rain_ when-ev-er I want it to._ And

Cm7 Ab add9

I can build a cas - tle from a sin-gle grain of sand and

Cm7 Ab add9 Bb/D

I can make a ship sail on dry land,

Fm Cm **To Coda**

but my life is in-com-plete and I'm so blue. 'Cause

Fm
Cm
I can't get next to you_
I can't get next to you_ babe, I

Fsus4
Cm
can't get next to you, I can't get next to you babe, I
1
Fsus
Cm7
can't get next to you.
(Instrumental)
A♭add9
Cm7
A♭add9
B♭/D
2
Fsus
can't get next to you, I
Cm7
can't get next to you babe, I
Fsus
can't get next to you.
(Instrumental)
Cm7
A♭add9
B♭

Cm7
Ab add9
Bb
3
Cm7
Ab add9
Bb
3
Cm7
Ab add9
Bb
D.C. al Coda
CODA
Fm
Cm
man, _
you're the key to my hap-pi-ness, 'cause

F
Bb/F
Fm7
F
Abmaj7
I

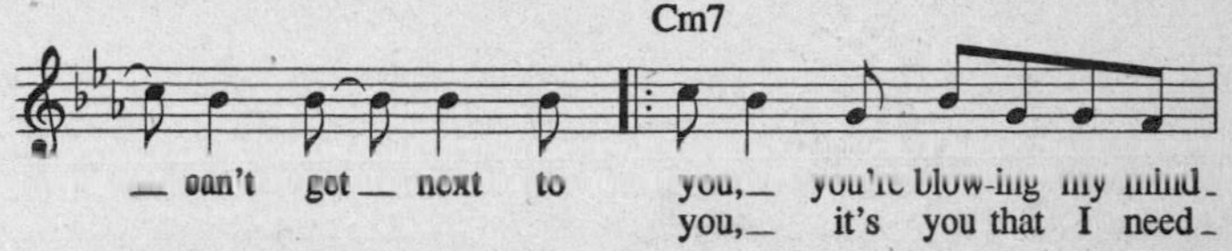
Cm7
can't get next to
you, you're blow-ing my mind
you, it's you that I need

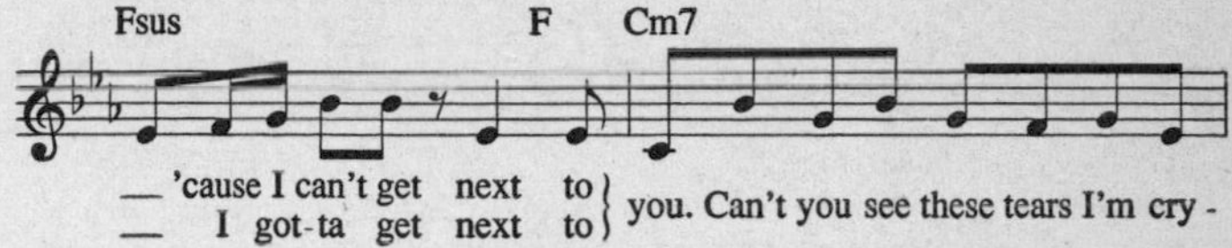
Fsus
F
Cm7
'cause I can't get next to
I got-ta get next to
you. Can't you see these tears I'm cry -

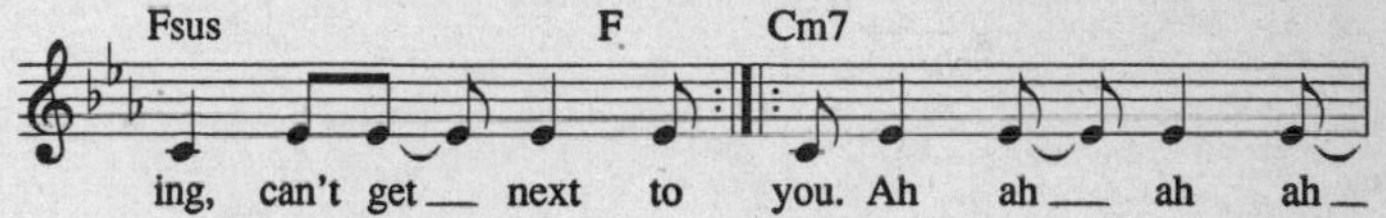
Fsus
F
Cm7
ing, can't get next to you. Ah ah ah ah

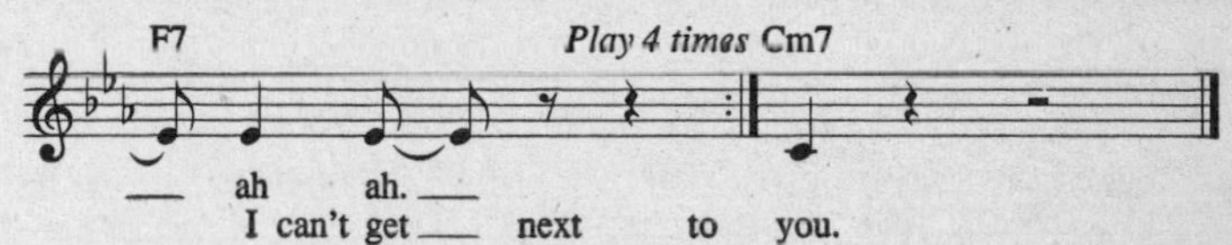
F7
Play 4 times
Cm7
ah ah.
I can't get next to you.

Additional Lyrics

2. I can fly like a bird in the sky
And I can buy anything that money can buy.
I can turn a river into a raging fire
I can live forever if I so desire.
I don't want it, all these things I can do
'Cause I can't get next to you.

3. I can turn back the hands of time - you better believe I can
I can make the seasons change just by waving my hand.
I can change anything from old to new
The thing I want to do the most I'm unable to do.
I'm an unhappy woman with all the powers I possess
'Cause man, you're the key to my happiness.

I CAN'T HELP MYSELF
(Sugar Pie, Honey Bunch)

Words and Music by BRIAN HOLLAND,
LAMONT DOZIER and EDWARD HOLLAND

leav - ing just your
But ev - 'ry time I
Dm
pic - ture be - hind
see your face
Em F
and I kissed it a thou - sand times.
I get all choked up in - side.
G
To Coda
C
When you snap your fin - ger or
When
wink your eye I come a - run - ning to you.
G
Dm
I'm tied to your a - pron strings
Em F
and there's noth - ing that I can do.

G
C
(Instrumental)

G
Can't

Dm
Em
help my - self, no I can't

F
G
D.C. al Coda
help my - self.

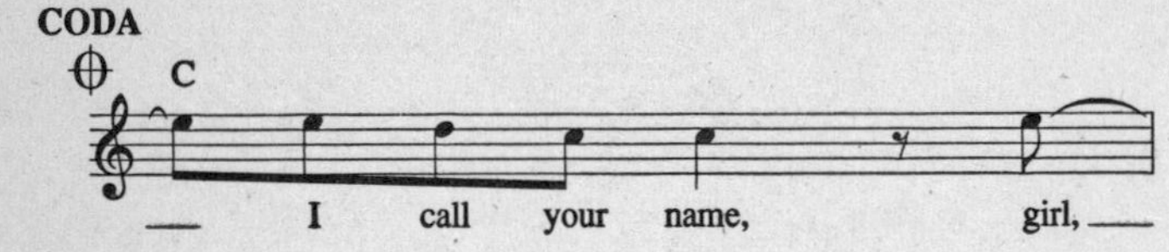
CODA
C
I call your name, girl,

it starts the flame burn -

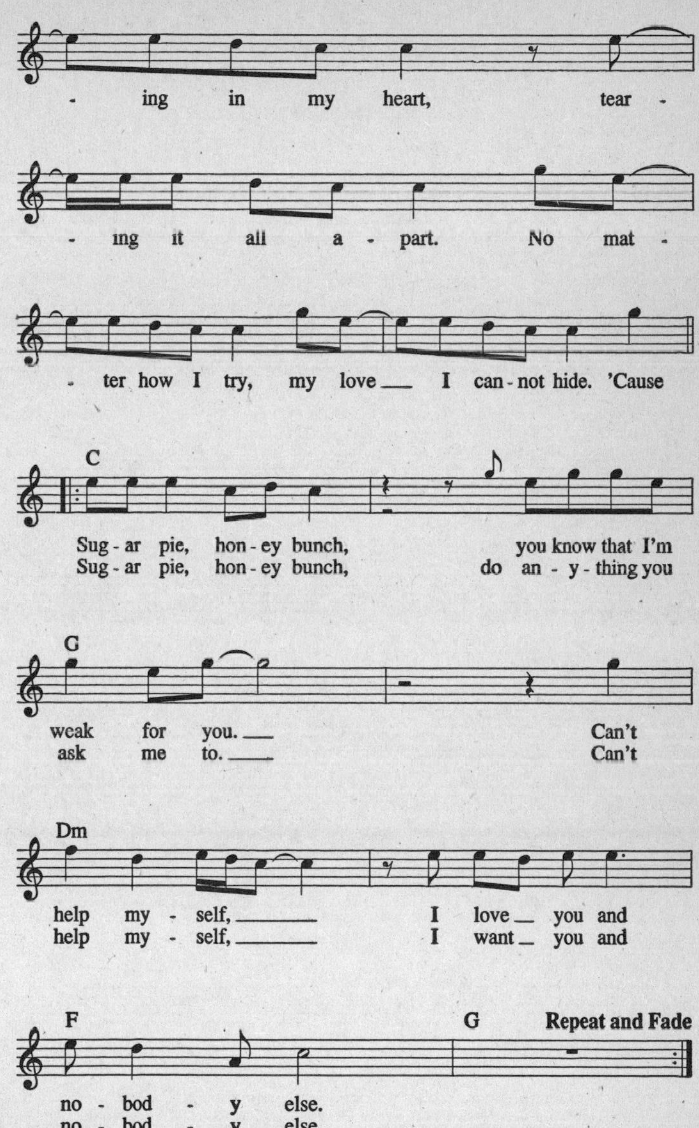
- ing in my heart, tear -
- ing it all a - part. No mat -
- ter how I try, my love ___ I can - not hide. 'Cause
C
Sug - ar pie, hon - ey bunch, you know that I'm
Sug - ar pie, hon - ey bunch, do an - y - thing you
G
weak for you. ___ Can't
ask me to. ___ Can't
Dm
help my - self, ___ I love ___ you and
help my - self, ___ I want ___ you and
F
G
Repeat and Fade
no - bod - y else.
no - bod - y else.

I HEAR A SYMPHONY

Words and Music by EDWARD HOLLAND,
LAMONT DOZIER and BRIAN HOLLAND

Am7
C
D7
clos - er, clos - er to your arms.
G
Then sud - den - ly, oo,
D/F#
your lips are touch - ing mine.
Dm/F
A feel - ing so di - vine
Am7
Cmaj7
D7
'Til I leave the past be - hind.
Cm
I'm lost in a world
B♭
Gm
Am7
made for you and me. Oo
G
B♭m7
E♭7
N.C.
love me. When-ev - er you are

A♭
near
I hear a
E♭/G
sym - pho - ny
play sweet and
E♭m/G♭
ten - der - ly
ev 'ry
B♭m
D♭
E7
time your lips meet mine my ba - by.
A
Ba - by, ba - by,
I feel a
E/G♯
joy with - in.
Don't let this
Em/G
feel - ing end.
Let it go
Bm
D
F7
on and on and on now ba - by.

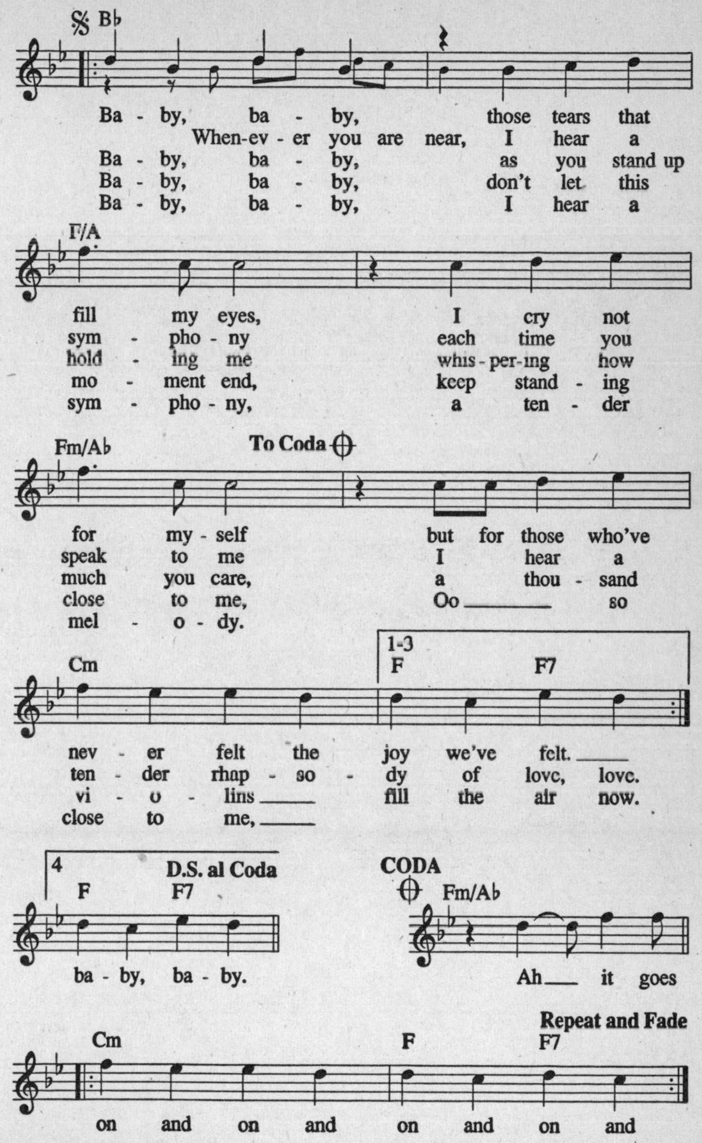

B♭
Ba - by, ba - by, those tears that
When-ev - er you are near, I hear a
Ba - by, ba - by, as you stand up
Ba - by, ba - by, don't let this
Ba - by, ba - by, I hear a
F/A
fill my eyes, I cry not
sym - pho - ny each time you
hold - ing me whis - per-ing how
mo - ment end, keep stand - ing
sym - pho - ny, a ten - der
Fm/A♭
To Coda
for my - self but for those who've
speak to me I hear a
much you care, a thou - sand
close to me, Oo so
mel - o - dy.
Cm
1-3
F
F7
nev - er felt the joy we've felt.
ten - der rhap - so - dy of love, love.
vi - o - lins fill the air now.
close to me,
4
D.S. al Coda
F
F7
ba - by, ba - by.
CODA
Fm/A♭
Ah it goes
Repeat and Fade
Cm
F
F7
on and on and on and on and

I SECOND THAT EMOTION

Words and Music by WILLIAM "SMOKEY" ROBINSON
and ALFRED CLEVELAND

G
A
taste of hon - ey's worse _ than none at all. ___
so it makes you wise ___ to break the rules._
D
Oh, ___ lit - tle girl, in
G
that case I don't want no part. ___
D
I do be - lieve ___ that
G
that would on - ly break ___ my heart. ___
D
Oh, ___ but if you feel like lov-in' me, _
A
G
if you got the no - tion, ___ I sec-ond that e -

D
mo - tion. So if you feel like giv-ing me a
A G
life - time of de - vo - tion,
D
To Coda
I sec - ond that e - mo - tion.
1
A G
May -
2
A G
(Instrumental)
D A G
D.S. al Coda
Oh lit - tle girl in
CODA
Repeat ad lib. and Fade
A G D
(Instrumental)

I'LL BE THERE

Words and Music by BERRY GORDY, HAL DAVIS, WILLIE HUTCH and BOB WEST

F
Fsus
F
be there.
(I'll be there.)
Ab
I'll be there to com -
Eb
- fort you,
build my world
Bb
of dreams a - round you.
F
3
I'm so glad I found you.
Ab
3
I'll be there with a love
Eb
so strong.
I'll be your strength,
To Coda
Bb
you know I'll keep

B♭/C
F
hold - ing on. Let me fill your heart
C/E
with joy and laugh - ter.
Dm
Dm/C
To - geth - er - ness,
Am7
well it's all I'm af - ter.
B♭
Gm7
3
B♭/C
Just call my name and I'll
F
C7sus
D.S. al Coda
be there.
(I'll be there.)
CODA
B♭/C
hold - ing on.
3

F
C/E
If you should ev - er find some - one new,
Dm
Dm/C
Am7
I know she'd bet - ter be good to you,
B♭
Gm7
3
B♭/C
'cause if she does - n't, then I'll
F
be there.
(I'll be there.
C7sus
Don't you know, ba - by.
F
I'll be there,
C/E
Dm
Dm/C
I'll be there.
Am7
B♭
Gm7
3
Just call my

B♭/C
name
and I'll

F
1
C7sus
be there.

2
Freely
B♭
Gm7
3
Just call my name

B♭/C
and I'll be there.

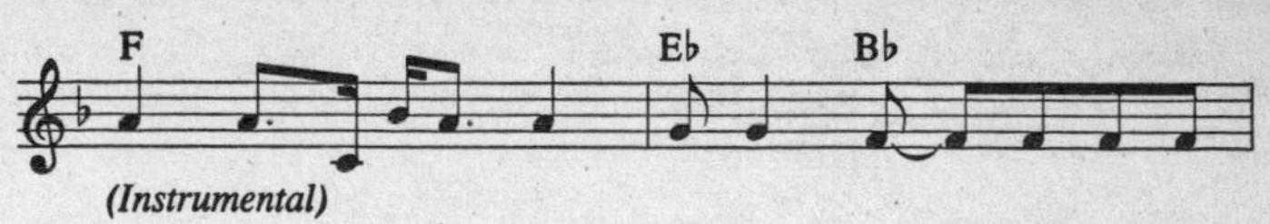
F
E♭
B♭
(Instrumental)

F
E♭
B♭

I WANT YOU BACK

Words and Music by FREDDIE PERREN, ALPHONSO MIZELL, BERRY GORDY and DEKE RICHARDS

Em G/B Cmaj7 G
Now it's much too late for me to
Fol - low - ing the girl I did - n't
Am7 D9 G
take a sec - ond look.
e - ven want a - round.
Oh, ba - by, give me one more chance
Oh, ba - by, all I need is one
C6 Am7 D9
to show you that I love you.
more chance to show you that I love you.
Em G/B Cmaj7 G Am9 D11 G
Won't you please let me back in your heart,
Won't you please let me back in your heart,
Oh, dar - ling, I was blind to
Oh, dar - ling, I was blind to
C Am7 D
1
Em7 G/B Cmaj7 G
let you go, but now since I see
let you go, but

Am
D11
G
you in his arms I want you back.
D11
G
I, I do now, I want you back.
D11
G
ooh, ooh, ba - by, I want you back.
C
D9
G
Yeah, yeah, yeah, I want you back.
C7
2
Em
G/B
Cmaj7
G
Hey, hey, now, now now since I see you
D
G
in his arms. Oh, oh.
(Instrumental)
Oh, just give me one more

C Am7 D11
chance to show you that I love you,
Em7 G/B C G Am D11 G
ba - by, ba - by, ba - by, For -
D11 G C7
get what hap - pened then. Let me live a -
G
gain, oh, ba - by, I was blind to
C6 Am7 D11
let you go, 'cause
Em G/B Cmaj7 G Am7 D11 G
now since I see you in his arms
D11 G
spare me of this cost.
C7 G D.S. and Fade
Give back what I lost.

I'M LOSING YOU
(I Know)

Words and Music by CORNELIUS GRANT, NORMAN WHITFIELD and EDWARD HOLLAND

Moderately bright
D
Your love is fad - in', I can
F/D
G/D
feel your love fad - in'. Wom-an, it's fad - in' a -
3
F/D
D
way from me. 'Cause your bash - ful touch has grown
F/D
cold, as if some-one else con-trolled your ver -
D
C/D
G/D
D
- y soul. I fooled my - self
long as I can. I can
feel the pres - ence of an - oth -

F
- er man. It's
D
F/D
there when you speak my name, it's just not the same
G/D
F/D
oh ___ hon - ey, I'm los - ing you. I can
D
F/D
feel it in _ the air, it's there ev-'ry-where, ___
G/D
Oh, ___ hon - ey I'm
F/D
los - ing you. I can
D
feel it in ___ my bones, _ an - y
look in - to ___ your eyes, ___ a re -

F/D
G/D
day you'll be up and gone.
Ooh,
I'm
flec - tion of a face I see.
Oh, Lord,
I'm
F/D
1
D
los - ing you.
It's all
o - ver your face,
some-one's
los - ing you.
I'm
F/D
tak - in' my place.
Could it
G/D
F/D
be
that I'm los - ing you?
When I
2
D
hurt,
down-heart-ed
and wor-ried, girl,
'cause that
face
does - n't be - long to me.
Ooh
Hm
hm
N.C.
hm
hm

D
hm. your love is fad - in',
F
I can feel it fad - in',
G/D
F/D
Oh a - way from me. I can
D
feel it in the air, it's
I don't wan - na lose you, but I
F/D
G/D
there ev - 'ry-where, ooh, I'm
know I'm gon - na groove you. Oh, Lord I'm
F/D
D
los - ing you.
los - ing you. Your love is fad - in',
F/D
I can feel it fad - in'
G/D
D
F
Oh Lord, I'm los - ing you.

IF I WERE YOUR WOMAN

Words and Music by LAVERNE WARE,
PAM SAWYER and CLAY McMURRAY

Moderately
Gm
If I were your wom - an
Edim
3
and you were my man,
B♭/F
you'd have no oth - er wom - an,
G7
3
3
you'd be weak as a lamb.
Cm7
If you had the strength
Gm
to walk out that door,
Cm7
my love would o - ver - rule my sense,

Gm
and I'd call you back for more, if I were your
E♭m
wom - an, if I were your
Gm
wom - an and you were my
B♭
E♭/B♭
man. Um, ba - by.
Gm
She tears you down dar - lin',
Life is so cra - zy,
Edim
3
says you're noth-ing at all.
a love is un - kind.
B♭/F
But, I'll pick you up, dar - ling,
Be-cause she came first, dar - ling,

G7
when she lets you fall.
will she hang on your mind?
Cm7
You're like a dia - mond
You're a part of me,
Gm
To Coda
but she treats you like glass.
and you don't e - ven know it.
Cm7
Yet you beg her to love you,
E♭m/G♭
but, me you don't ask. If I were your
B♭
wom - an, if I were your
E♭m/B♭
wom - an, if I were your
B♭/F
wom - an, here's what I'd

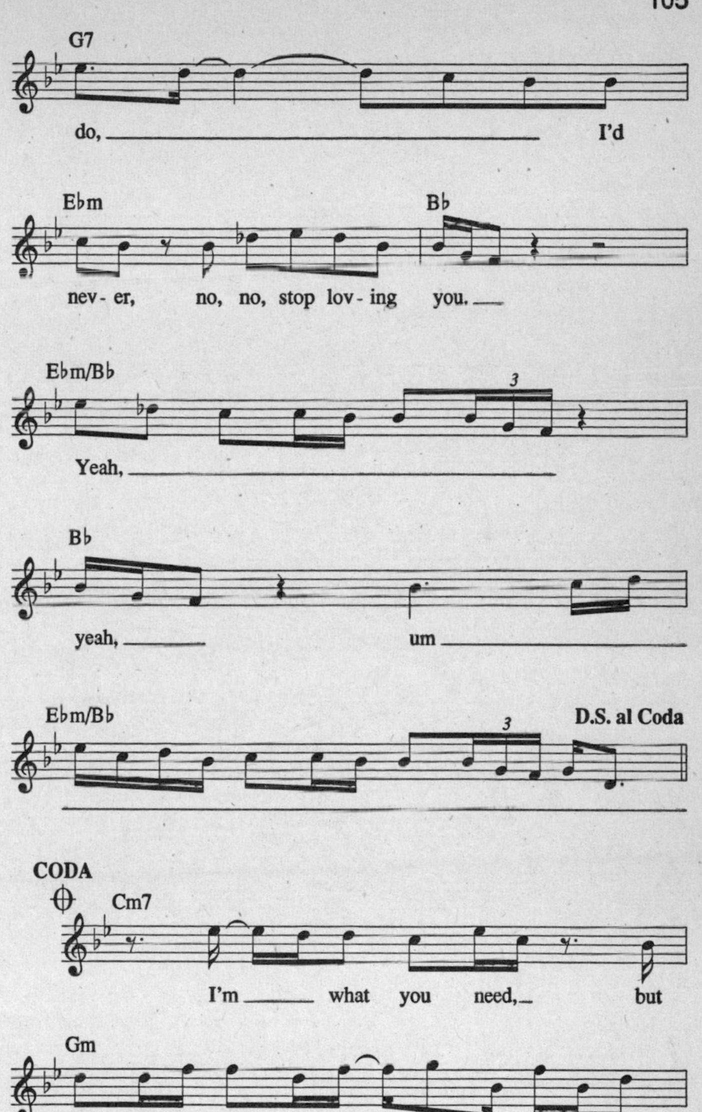
G7
do, I'd
Ebm
Bb
nev - er, no, no, stop lov - ing you.
Ebm/Bb
3
Yeah,
Bb
yeah, um
Ebm/Bb
3
D.S. al Coda
CODA
Cm7
I'm what you need, but
Gm
I'm too a - fraid to show it. If I were your

Bb
wom - an, if I were
Ebm/Bb
your wom - an, if I were your
Bb
wom - an, here's what I'd
wom - an, here's what I'd
G7
do.
do.
Ebm
Nev - er, no, no, no, stop lov - ing
Nev - er, nev - er stop lov - ing you if
Bb
you, ah,
I were your woman,
Ebm/Bb
Repeat and Fade
yeah. If I were your
your sweet loving woman.

JUST MY IMAGINATION

(Running Away with Me)

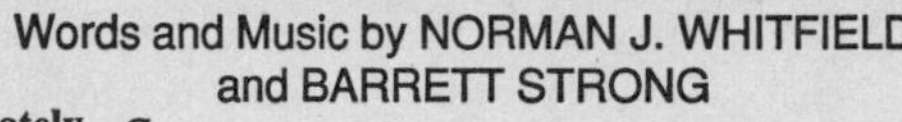

Words and Music by NORMAN J. WHITFIELD
and BARRETT STRONG

Moderately

G
Each day through my win - dow I
Soon, soon we'll be

Am7 G
watch her as she pass - es by. ___
mar - ried and raise a fam - i - ly. ___

Am7 G
I say to my - self; "You are
A co - zy lit-tle home out in

Am7 G
such ___ a luck - y guy." ___
the coun - try with two chil - dren, maybe three.

Am7 G
To have a girl like her ___
I tell you I

Am7 G
___ is tru - ly a dream come ___ true. ___
can vi - sual - ize it ___ all. ___

Am7
G
Out of all the fel - lows in the
This could - n't be a dream, for
Am7
G
world, she be - longs to me.
too real it all seems.
Am7
G
But it was just my i-mag - in - a - tion
Am7
G
run-nin' a - way with me,
Am7
G
It was just my i-mag - in - a - tion
Am7
G
run - nin' a - way with me.
1
Am7
2
G
D
C
G
Ev - 'ry night on my

knees__ I pray,__
dear Lord,__ hear my plea.__
Don't ev - er let an - oth - er
take her love from me or I would
D7
sure - ly die.__ Her love is
G
heav - en - ly. When her arms en - fold me,
I hear a ten - der rhap - so - dy. But in re -
D.S. and Fade
al - i - ty, she does - n't e - ven know me.

IF YOU REALLY LOVE ME

Words and Music by STEVIE WONDER
and SYREETA WRIGHT

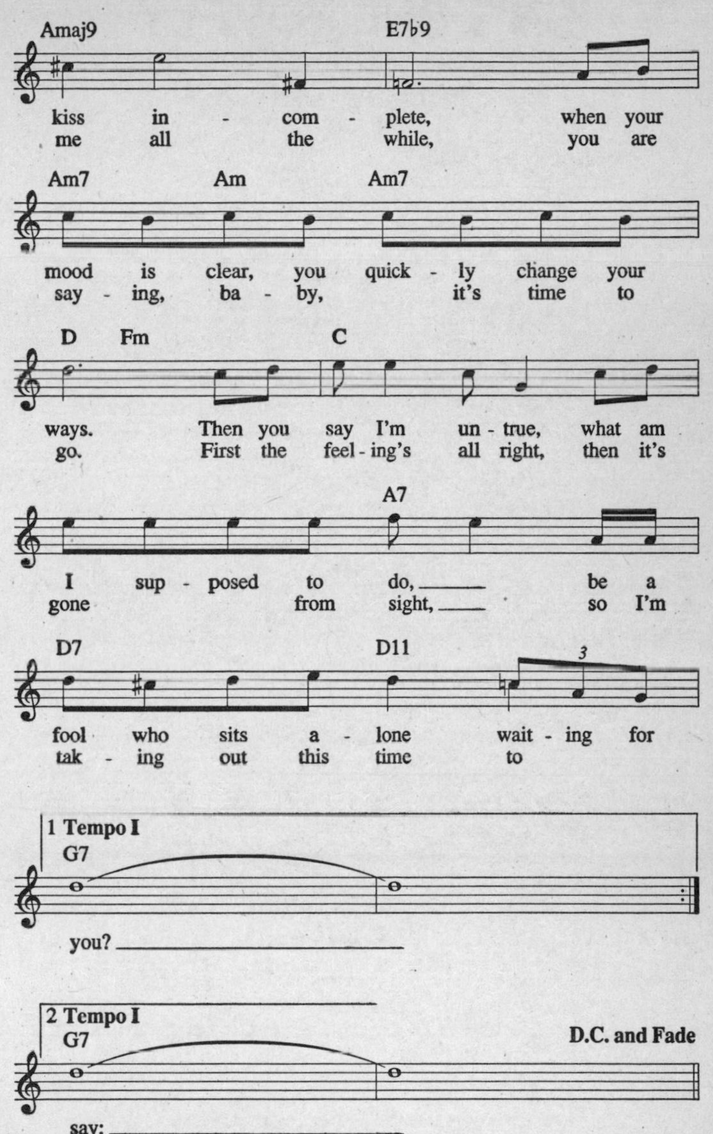
Amaj9
E7♭9
kiss in - com - plete, when your
me all the while, you are
Am7
Am
Am7
mood is clear, you quick - ly change your
say - ing, ba - by, it's time to
D
Fm
C
ways. Then you say I'm un - true, what am
go. First the feel - ing's all right, then it's
A7
I sup - posed to do, ___ be a
gone from sight, ___ so I'm
D7
D11
3
fool who sits a - lone wait - ing for
tak - ing out this time to
1 Tempo I
G7
you? ___
2 Tempo I
G7
D.C. and Fade
say: ___

ISN'T SHE LOVELY

Words and Music by
STEVIE WONDER

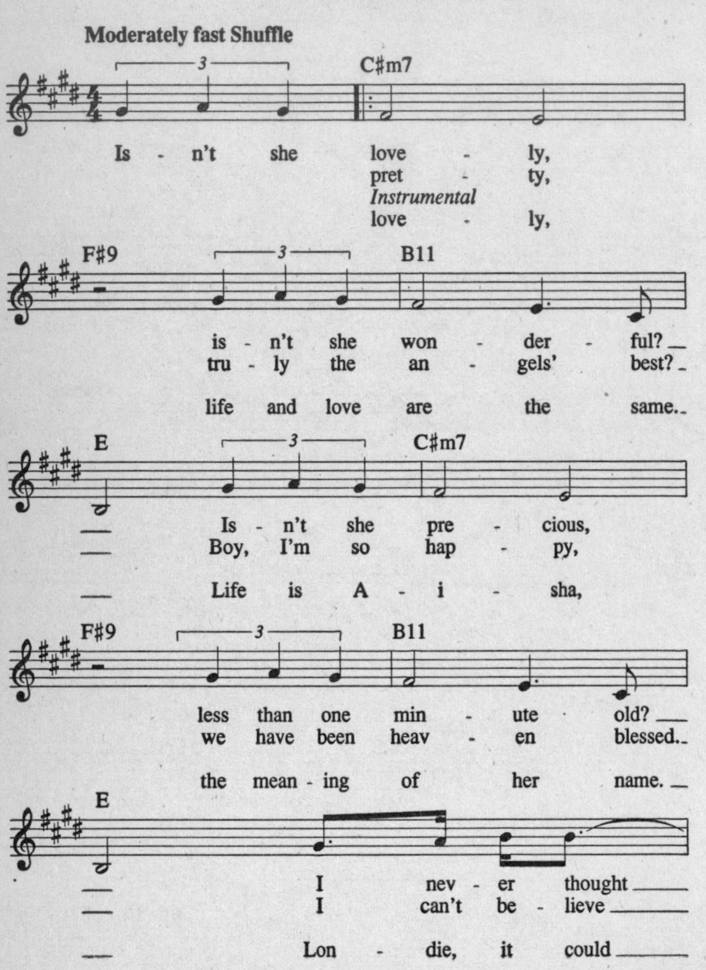

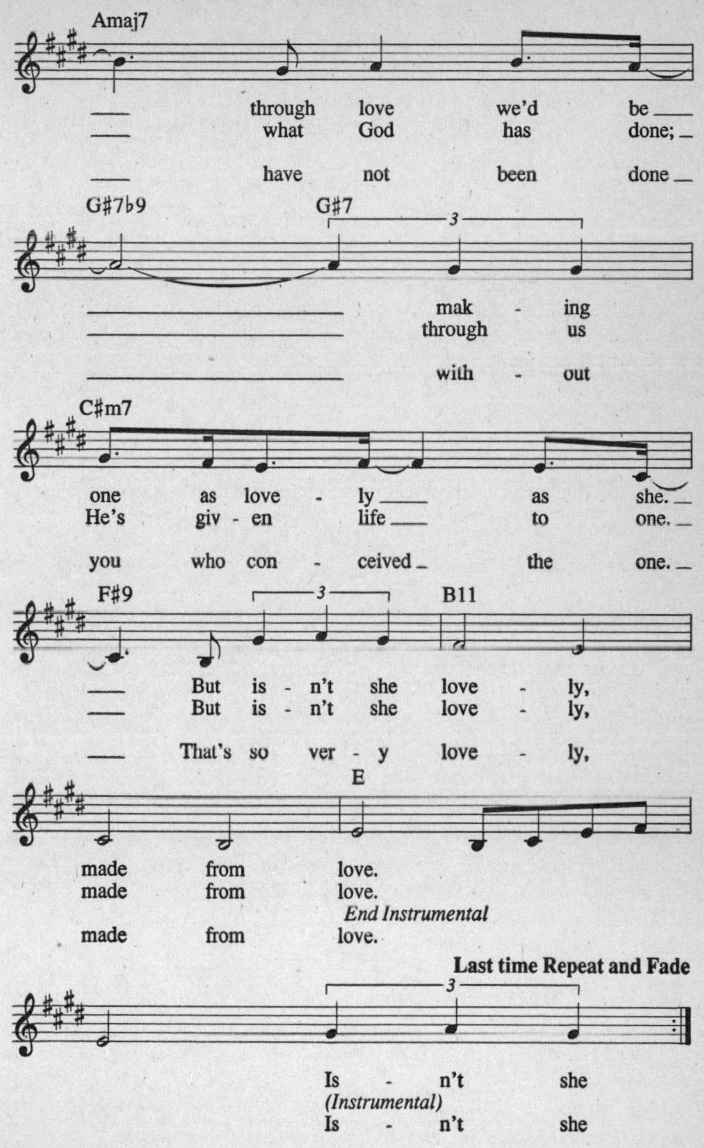
Amaj7
through love we'd be
what God has done;
have not been done
G#7♭9
G#7
3
mak - ing
through us
with - out
C#m7
one as love - ly as she.
He's giv - en life to one.
you who con - ceived the one.
F#9
3
B11
But is - n't she love - ly,
But is - n't she love - ly,
That's so ver - y love - ly,
E
made from love.
made from love.
End Instrumental
made from love.
Last time Repeat and Fade
3
Is - n't she
(Instrumental)
Is - n't she

IT'S THE SAME OLD SONG

Words and Music by EDWARD HOLLAND,
LAMONT DOZIER and BRIAN HOLLAND

F
G
night long. It used to
we used to be. Keep
C
bring sweet mem - o - ries of a
hear - ing the part that used to touch our heart say - ing to -
Dm
F
G
ten - der love that used to be, now it's the
geth - er for - ev - er. Break-ing up nev - er, it's the
C
G
same old song but with a
Instrumental
Dm
dif - f'rent mean - ing since - a
G
F
you been gone. Now it's the
C
G
same, same old song but with a

Dm
dif - f'rent mean - ing since - a
G F To Coda C
1
you been gone.
(3rd time) Precious
I, oh I,
2
sen - ti - men - tal (Instrumental)
(D.S. Instrumental)
3
mem - o - ries keep - a lin - ger - ing on,
Dm
ev - 'ry - time I hear our
F G
fa - vo - rite song, now you're
C
gone, left this emp - ti - ness, I

Dm
on - ly re - mi - nisce. The
F G
hap - pi - ness we spent, we used to
C
dance to the mu - sic make ro -
Dm F D.S. al Coda
mance to the mu - sic, now it's the
CODA
C
I oh, I
G
can't bear to hear it, it's the same old
Dm
song but with a dif - f'rent mean - ing since
G F Repeat and Fade
you been gone. It's the

LIVING FOR THE CITY

Words and Music by
STEVIE WONDER

Moderately
G Am/G Gm7 Am/G
1. A boy is born in Hard-time, Mis-si-sip-pi,
2.-4. See additional lyrics
G Am/G Gm7 Am/G
sur-round-ed by four walls that ain't so pret-ty.
G Am/G Gm7 Am/G
His par-ents give him love and af-fec-tion
G Am/G Gm7 Am/G
to keep him strong, mov-in' in the right di-rec-tion. Liv-ing
C D D7
just e-nough, just e-nough for the cit-
G Am/G Gm7 1,3 Am/G 2,4 Am/G
-y. Da Ba Da

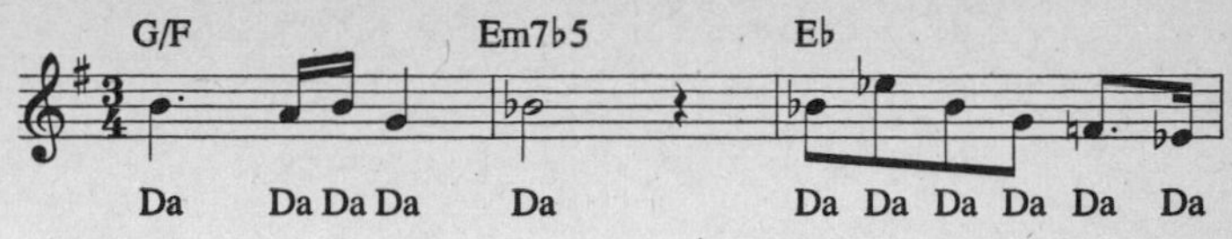

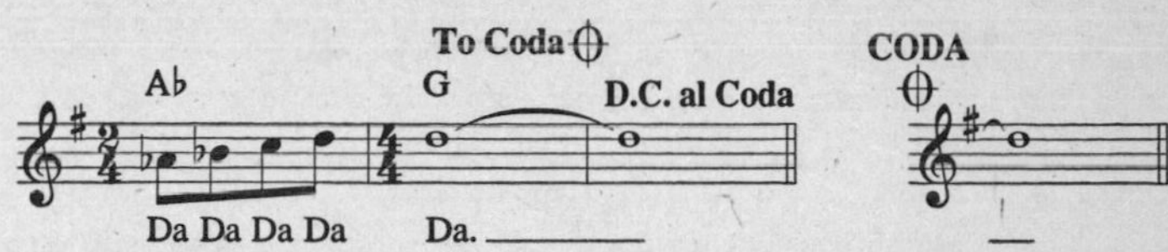

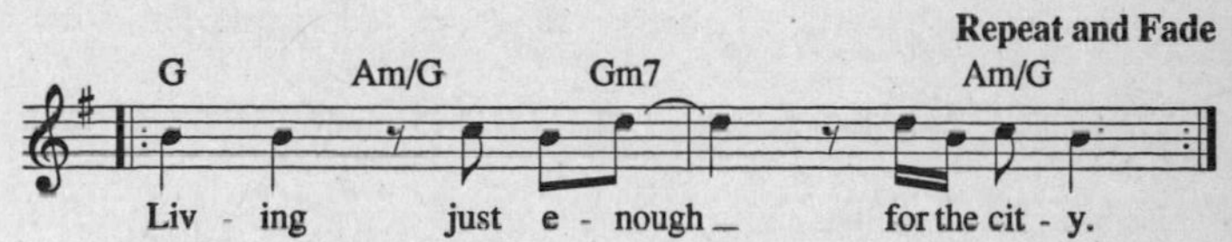

Additional Lyrics

2. His father works some days for fourteen hours,
And you can bet he barely makes a dollar.
His mother goes to scrub the floors for many,
And you'd best believe she hardly gets a penny.
Living just enough, just enough for the city.

3. His sister's black, but she is sho'nuff pretty.
Her skirt is short, but Lord her legs are sturdy.
To walk to school, she's got to get up early.
Her clothes are old, but never are they dirty.
Living just enough, just enough for the city.

4. Her brother's smart, he's got more sense than many.
His patience's long, but soon he won't have any.
To find a job is like a haystack, needle, 'cause
Where he lives, they don't use colored people.
Living just enough, just enough for the city.

THE LOVE YOU SAVE

Words and Music by BERRY GORDY, ALPHONSO MIZELL,
FREDDIE PERREN and DENNIS LUSSIER

Moderately

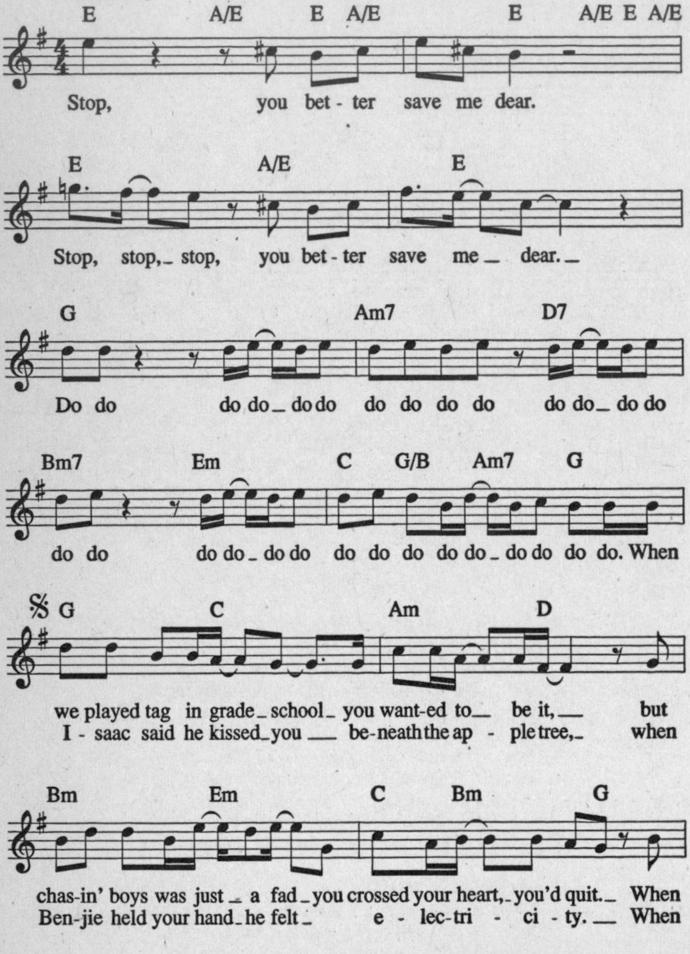

E A/E E A/E E A/E E A/E
Stop, you bet - ter save me dear.
E A/E E
Stop, stop, stop, you bet - ter save me dear.
G Am7 D7
Do do do do do do do do do do do do do do do
Bm7 Em C G/B Am7 G
do do do do do do do do do do do do do do do do. When
G C Am D
we played tag in grade school you want-ed to be it, but
I - saac said he kissed you be-neath the ap - ple tree, when
Bm Em C Bm G
chas-in' boys was just a fad you crossed your heart, you'd quit. When
Ben-jie held your hand he felt e - lec-tri - ci - ty. When

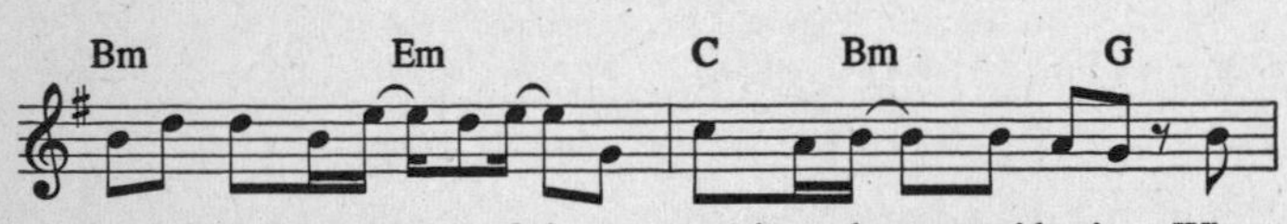

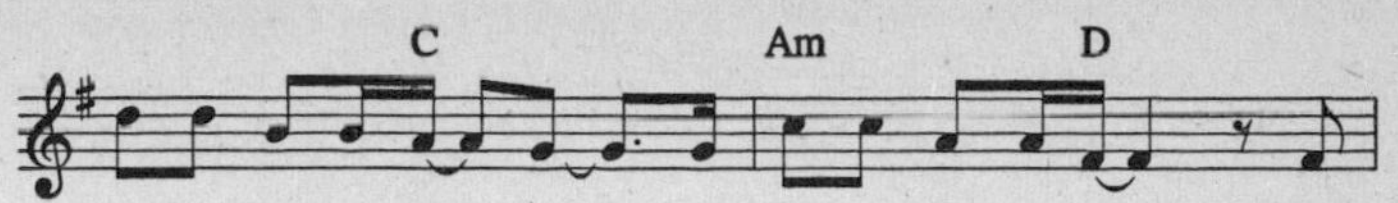
C Am D
we grew up you trad - ed your prom-ise for my ring: now
Al - ex - an - der called you he said he rang your chimes.

Bm Em C Bm G
just like back in grade school you're do-in' that same old thing.
Chris-to-pher dis-cov - ered you're way a - head of your time.

C Am Bm C D7sus
Stop, the love you save may be your own dar-lin' take it

Bm7 Em C Bm Am D
slow or some day you'll be all a - lone. You bet - ter

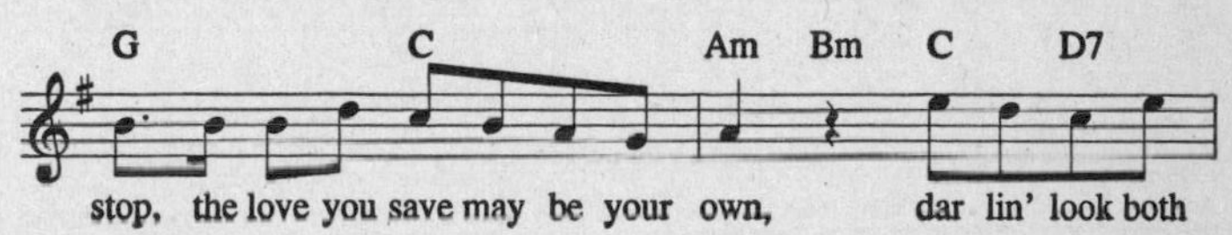
G C Am Bm C D7
stop, the love you save may be your own, dar lin' look both

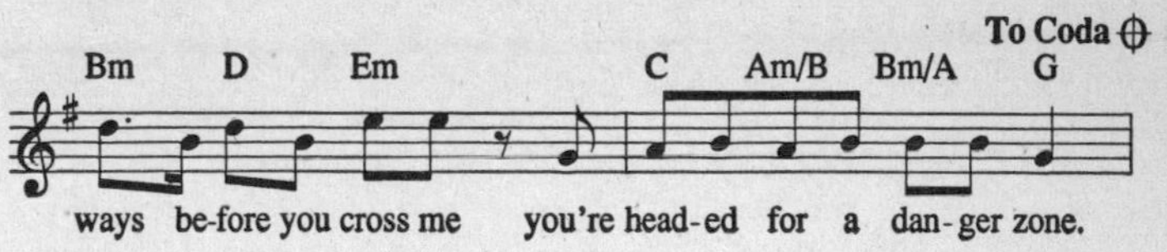
To Coda
Bm D Em C Am/B Bm/A G
ways be-fore you cross me you're head-ed for a dan-ger zone.

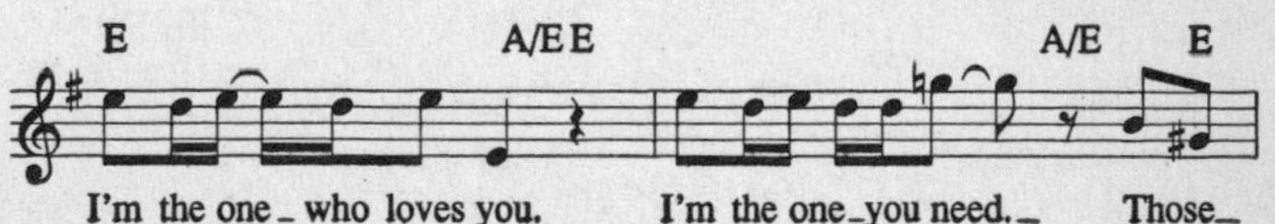
E A/E E A/E E
I'm the one who loves you. I'm the one you need. Those

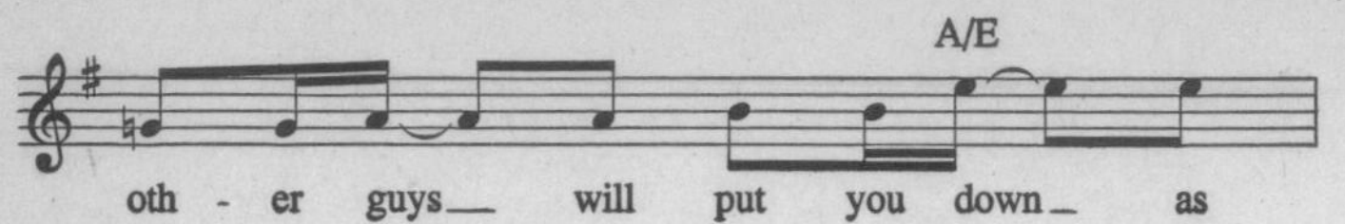
A/E
oth - er guys will put you down as

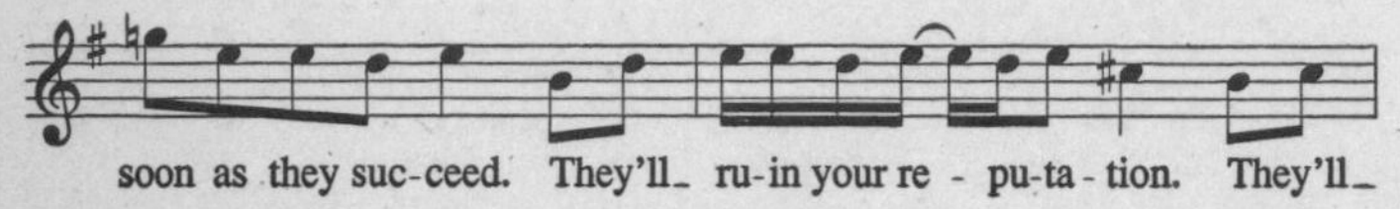
soon as they suc-ceed. They'll ru-in your re - pu-ta - tion. They'll

E
la - bel you a flirt. The

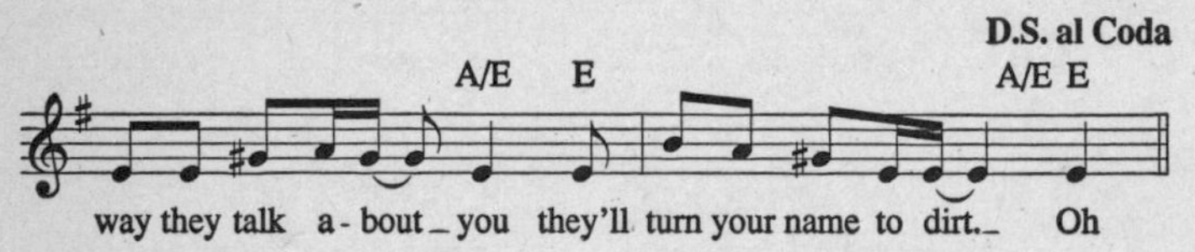
D.S. al Coda
A/E E
A/E E
way they talk a - bout you they'll turn your name to dirt. Oh

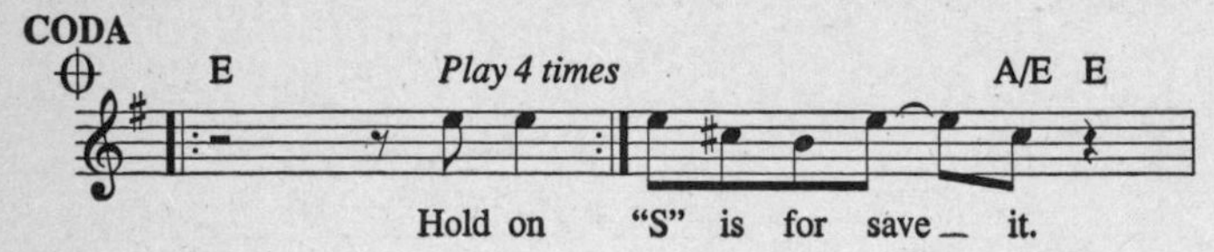
CODA
E
Play 4 times
A/E E
Hold on "S" is for save it.

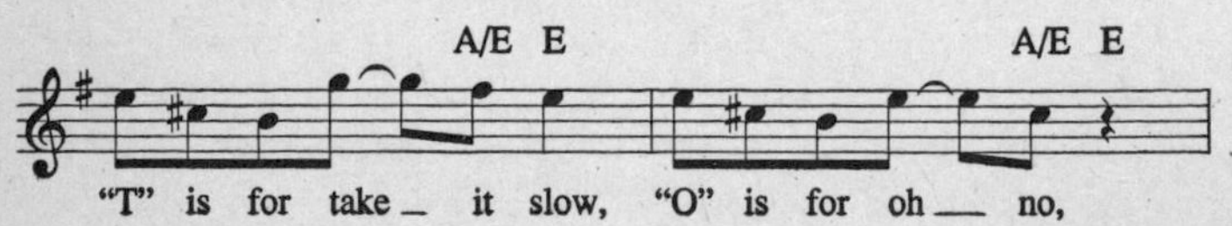
A/E E
A/E E
"T" is for take it slow, "O" is for oh no,

G
C
"P" is for please, please don't go; the love you save may be_your

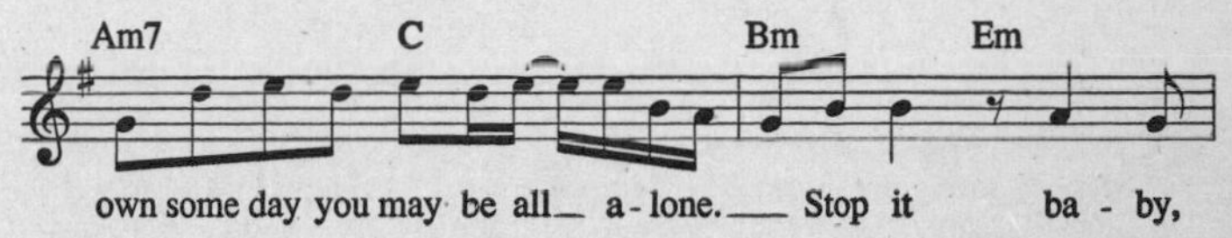
Am7
C
Bm
Em
own some day you may be all_ a - lone.___ Stop it ba - by,

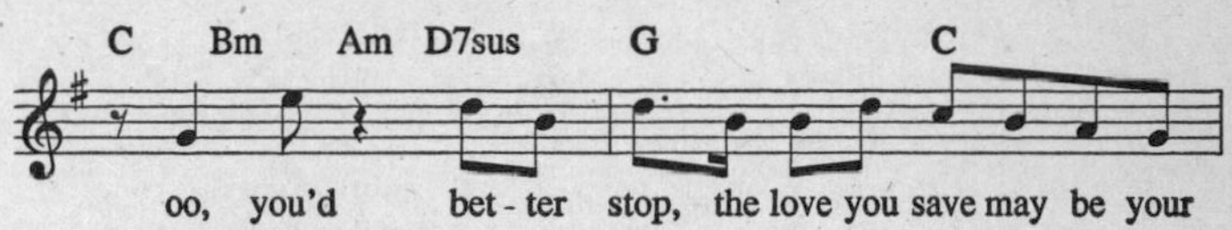
C
Bm
Am
D7sus
G
C
oo, you'd bet - ter stop, the love you save may be your

Am
Bm
C
D7
Bm
D
Em
own please, please oh, stop you, stop you ba - by you'll be

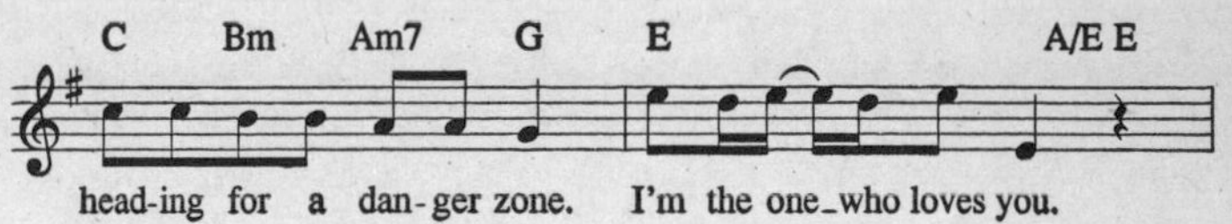
C
Bm
Am7
G
E
A/E E
head-ing for a dan-ger zone. I'm the one_who loves you.

A/E
E
I'm the one___ you need.________ Those___

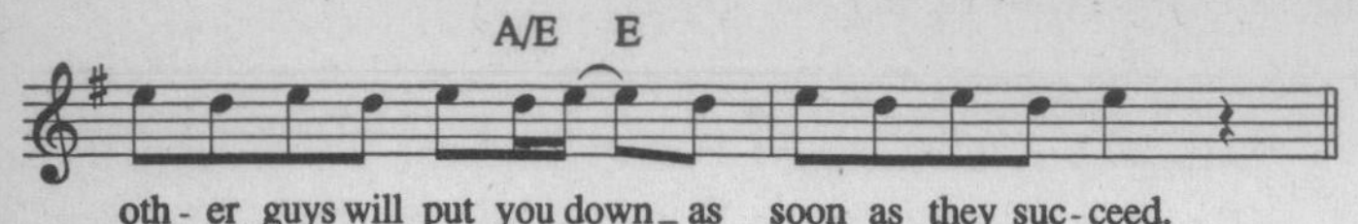
A/E E
oth - er guys will put you down _ as soon as they suc - ceed.

G C Am Em C
Stop, the love you save may be your own, you bet - ter
Stop, the love you save may be your own, don't you know don't you know

Bm D Em C Bm Am7 G
Stop it, stop it, stop it, girl, _ or some-day you'll be all a - lone. _
Stop it ba - by ___ or some-day you'll be all a - lone. _

N.C.

The way they talk _ a - bout _ you they'll
Those oth - er guys - will put _ you down as

Repeat and Fade
turn your name _ to, turn your name to
soon as they ___ suc - ceed.

MAMA'S PEARL

Words and Music by FREDDIE PERREN,
ALPHONSO MIZELL, BERRY GORDY and DEKE RICHARDS

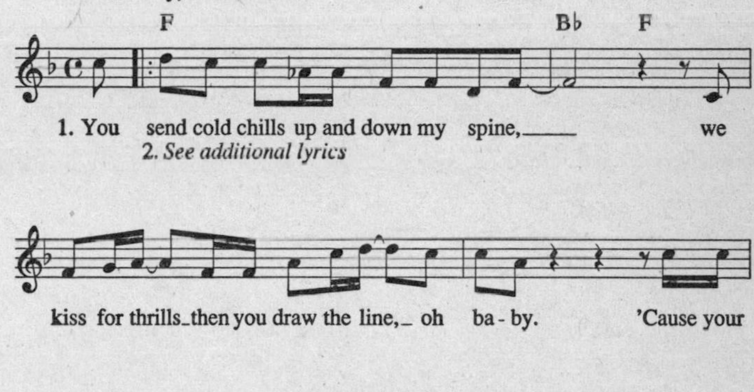
Moderately, with a beat
F
Bb
F
1. You send cold chills up and down my spine, we
2. See additional lyrics
kiss for thrills then you draw the line, oh ba - by. 'Cause your

Bb
F
ma-ma told you that love ain't right, But don't you

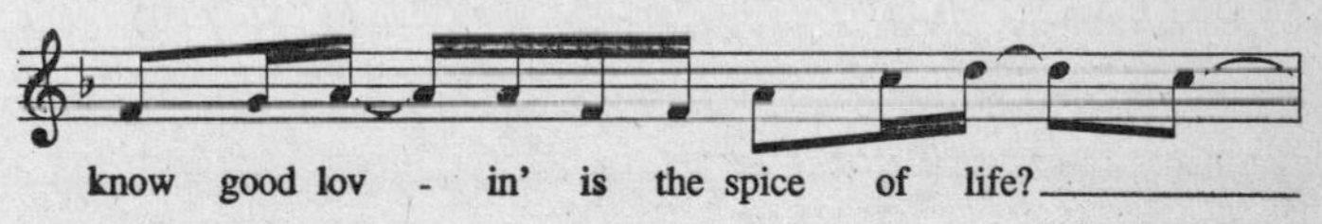
know good lov - in' is the spice of life?

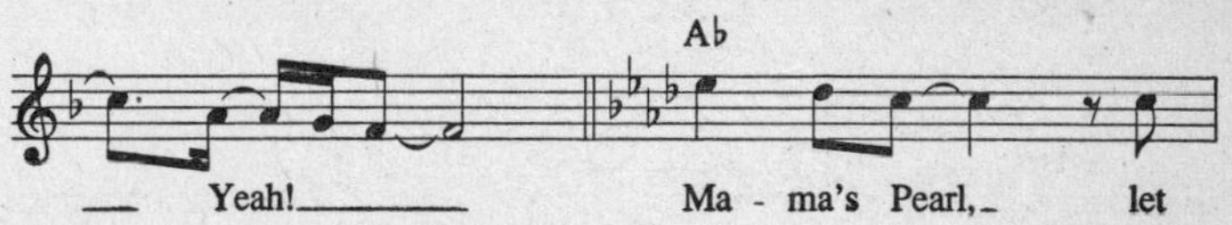
Ab
Yeah! Ma - ma's Pearl, let

Db
Eb
Ab
down those curls,_won't you give my love a whirl?_Find what _ you been

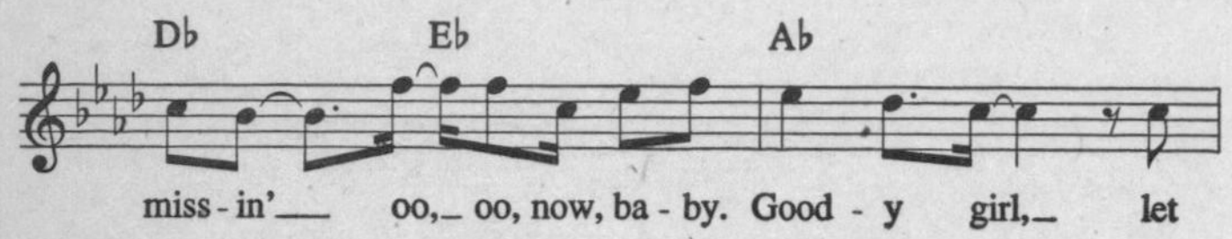
Db
Eb
Ab
miss - in'___ oo,_ oo, now, ba - by. Good - y girl,_ let

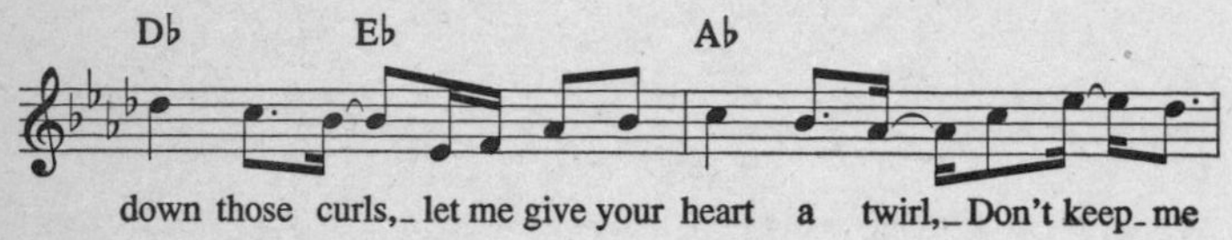
Db
Eb
Ab
down those curls,_let me give your heart a twirl,_Don't keep_me

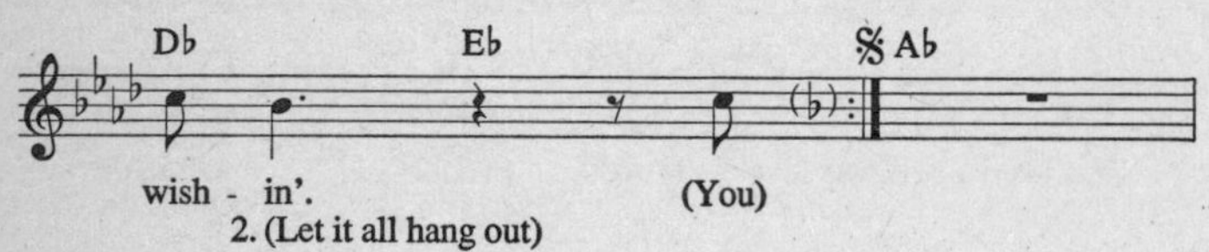
Db
Eb
Ab
wish - in'. (You)
2. (Let it all hang out)

Db
Eb
Let's fall in love,_ let's fall in love,_

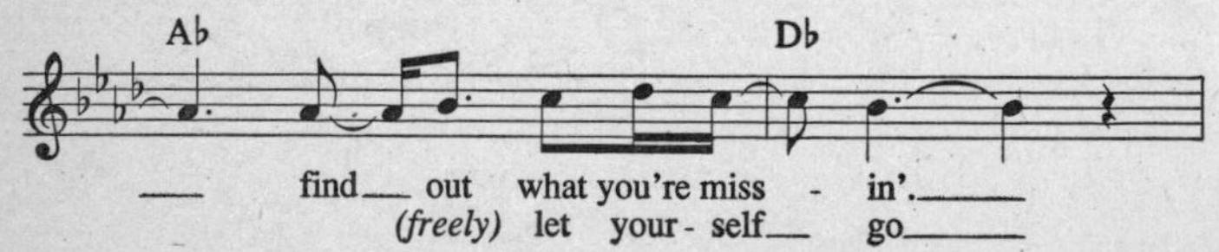
Ab
Db
___ find_ out what you're miss - in'.___
(freely) let your - self_ go___

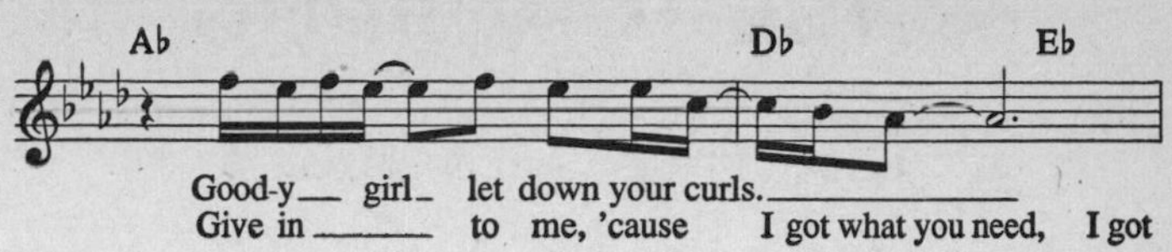

Ab
Db
Eb
Good-y girl let down your curls.
Give in to me, 'cause I got what you need, I got

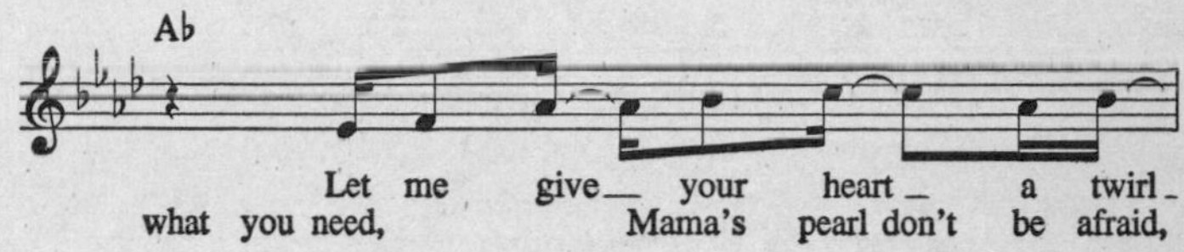

Ab
Let me give your heart a twirl
what you need, Mama's pearl don't be afraid,

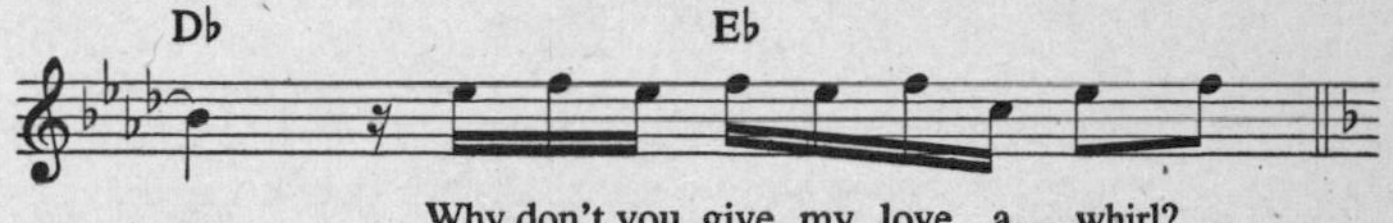

Db
Eb
Why don't you give my love a whirl?
daddy's girl, we got it made.

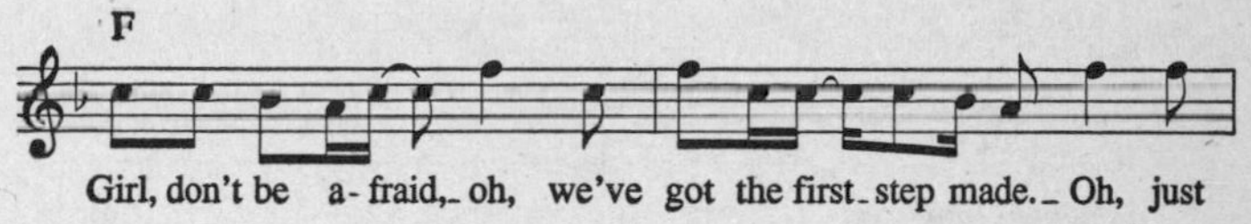

F
Girl, don't be a-fraid, oh, we've got the first step made. Oh, just

D.S. and Fade
give in, just give in to me 'cause I got what you need.

Additional Lyrics

2. You want my lovin', yes you do, do, do.
   You know my lovin' is true, true, now, baby.
   But your conscience tells you that love is wrong
   But just a little bit of lovin' never hurt no one.
   Oh,

MAYBE TOMORROW

Words and Music by BERRY GORDY, ALPHONSO J. MIZELL,
FREDERICK J. PERREN and DENNIS LUSSIER

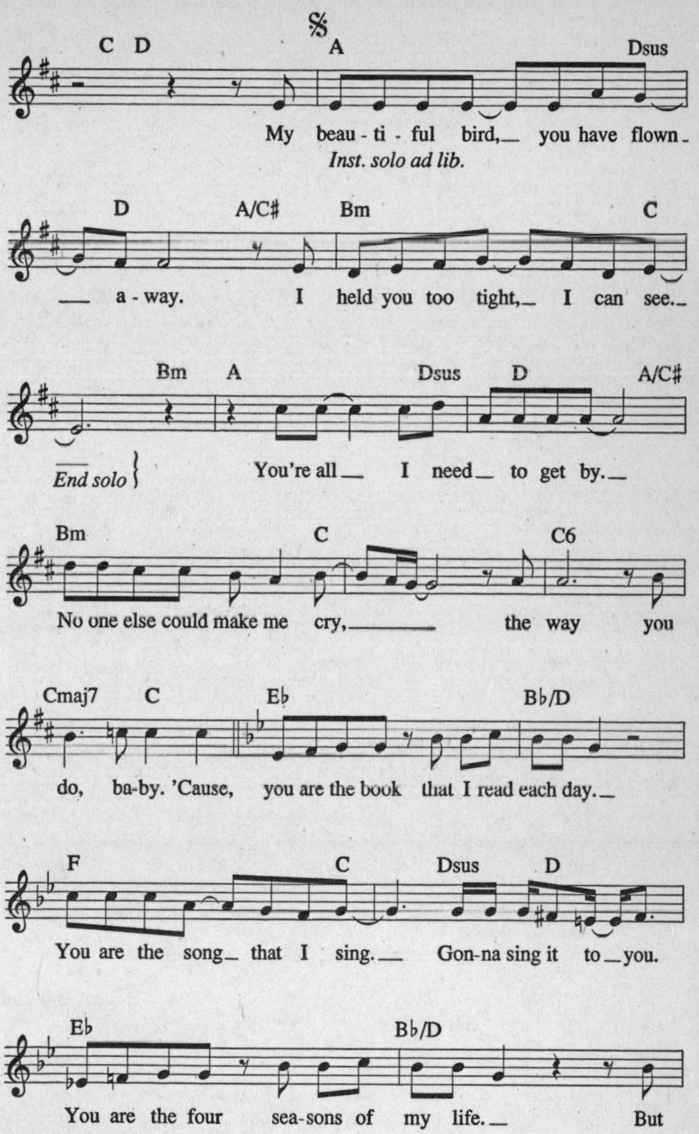

𝄋

C D A Dsus

My beau - ti - ful bird, you have flown

Inst. solo ad lib.

D A/C# Bm C

a - way. I held you too tight, I can see.

Bm A Dsus D A/C#

End solo } You're all I need to get by.

Bm C C6

No one else could make me cry, the way you

Cmaj7 C E♭ B♭/D

do, ba-by. 'Cause, you are the book that I read each day.

F C Dsus D

You are the song that I sing. Gon-na sing it to you.

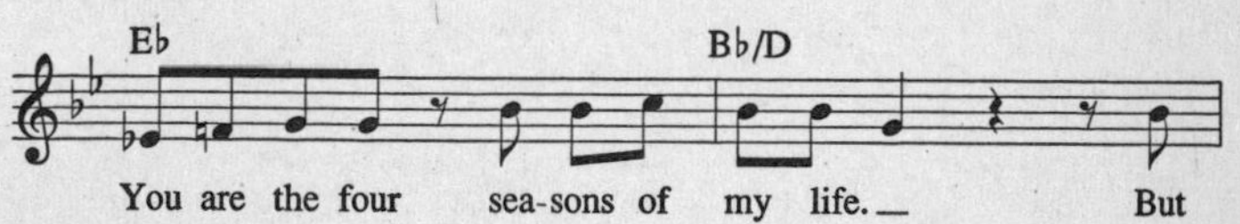

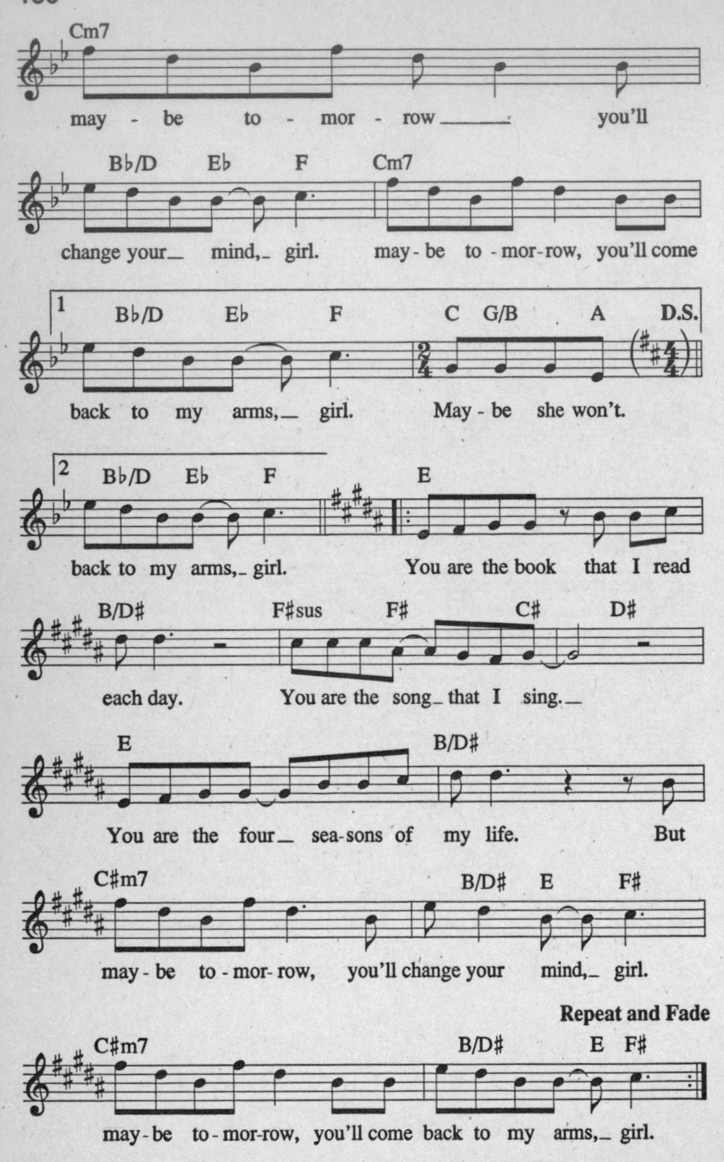
Cm7
may - be to - mor - row ___ you'll
B♭/D E♭ F Cm7
change your ___ mind, _ girl. may - be to - mor - row, you'll come
1
B♭/D E♭ F C G/B A D.S.
back to my arms, ___ girl. May - be she won't.
2
B♭/D E♭ F E
back to my arms, _ girl. You are the book that I read
B/D♯ F♯sus F♯ C♯ D♯
each day. You are the song _ that I sing. ___
E B/D♯
You are the four _ sea-sons of my life. But
C♯m7 B/D♯ E F♯
may - be to - mor - row, you'll change your mind, _ girl.
Repeat and Fade
C♯m7 B/D♯ E F♯
may - be to - mor - row, you'll come back to my arms, _ girl.

MONEY
(That's What I Want)

Words and Music by BERRY GORDY
and JANIE BRADFORD

Heavy Rock
Em
A
Em
A
Em
(Instrumental)
A
Em
A
Em
B
A(add2)
E
B
Em
B
1. The best things in life are free,
2. Your lov - in' gives me a thrill,
3.,4. Mon - ey don't get ev - 'ry - thing it's true,

Em
but you can keep 'em for the birds and bees;_ Now give me
but your lov - in' don't pay my bills;_ Now give me
what it don't get I ___ can't use;_ Now give me
A
mon - ey, that's what I
Em A Em B7
want, that's what I want ___
A7 Em A
4th time
To Coda
— yeah, ___ that's what I want._
1,2
Em B7
3
Em B7 D.C. (to intro) al Coda
CODA
Em B7
— Well, ___ now give me

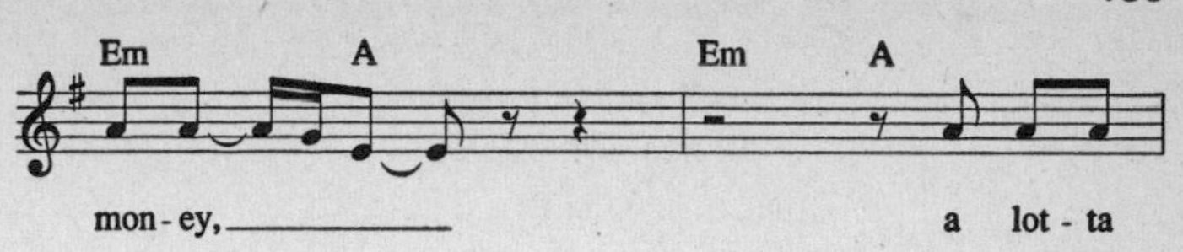
Em
A
Em
A
mon - ey,
a lot - ta

Em
A
Em
A
mon - ey,
Oh, yeah, I wan -
Wo, yeah, you need

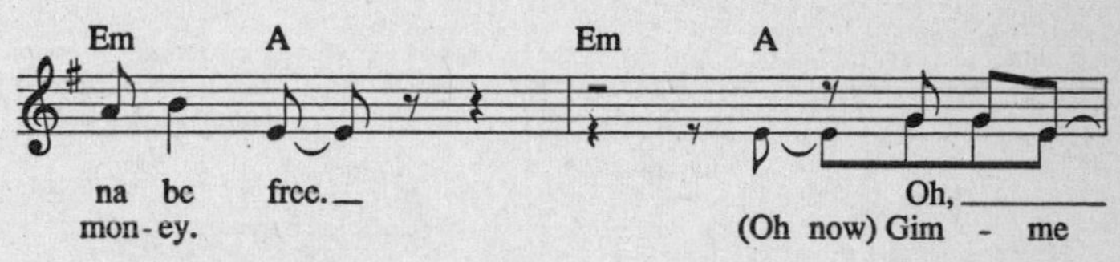
Em
A
Em
A
na be free.
mon - ey.
Oh,
(Oh now) Gim - me

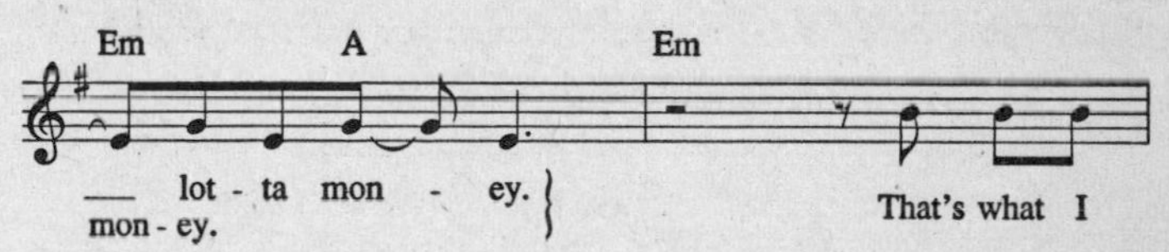
Em
A
Em
lot - ta mon - ey.
mon - ey.
That's what I

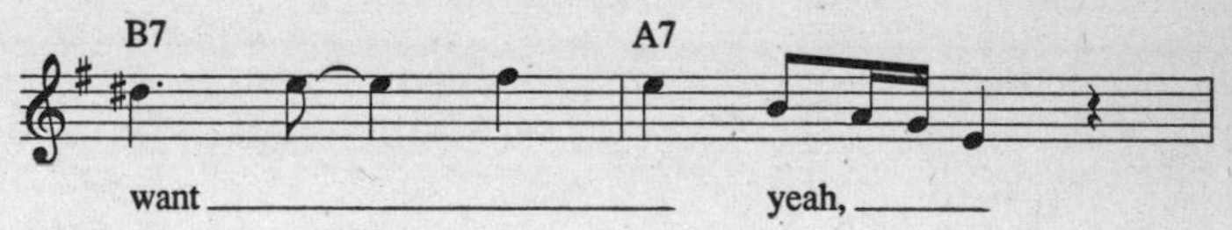
B7
A7
want
yeah,

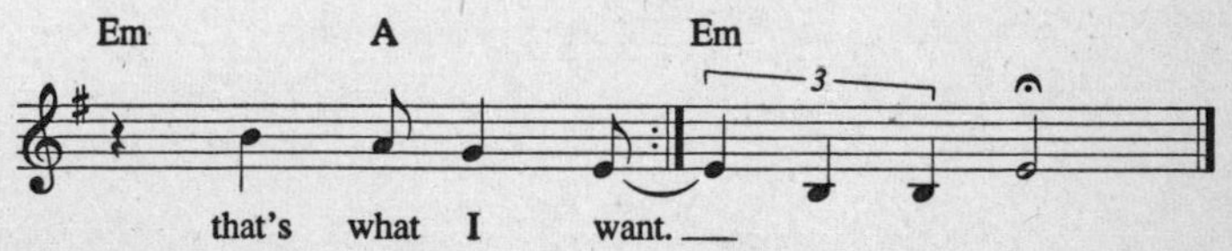
Em
A
Em
3
that's what I want.

MERCY, MERCY ME

(The Ecology)

Words and Music by
MARVIN GAYE

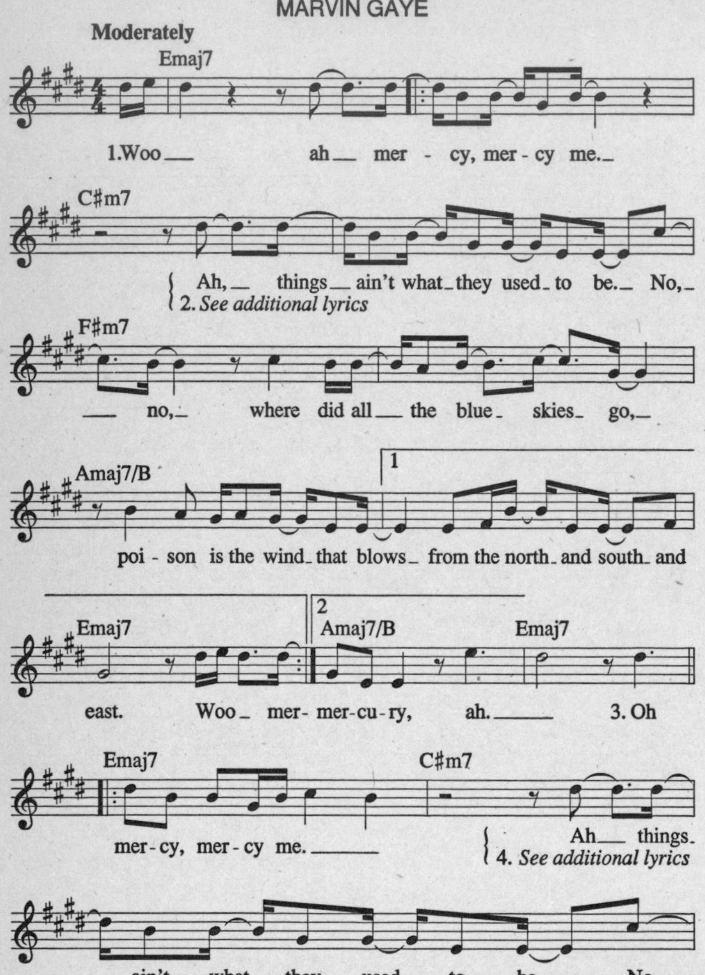

F♯m7
— no, no, ra - di-a - tion un - der-ground and in the_
Amaj7/B
1
— sky; — an - i - mals_ and birds who live near-by are
E
Emaj7
2
Amaj7/B
dy-ing. Oh, land _ how_ much more _ a - buse from man_
Emaj7
— can she stand?_ Oh — na, — na, —
D♭m7
F♯m7
3
my sweet _ Lord, no, no, na, na, na, —
Amaj7/B
— my, my Lord my — sweet Lord. _

Additional Lyrics

2. Ah things ain't what they used to be, no, no
Oil wasted on the ocean and upon
Our seas fish full of mercury, ah.

4. Ah things ain't what they used to be
What about this overcrowded land
How much more abuse from man can she stand?

MY CHERIE AMOUR

Words and Music by STEVIE WONDER, SYLVIA MOY and HENRY COSBY

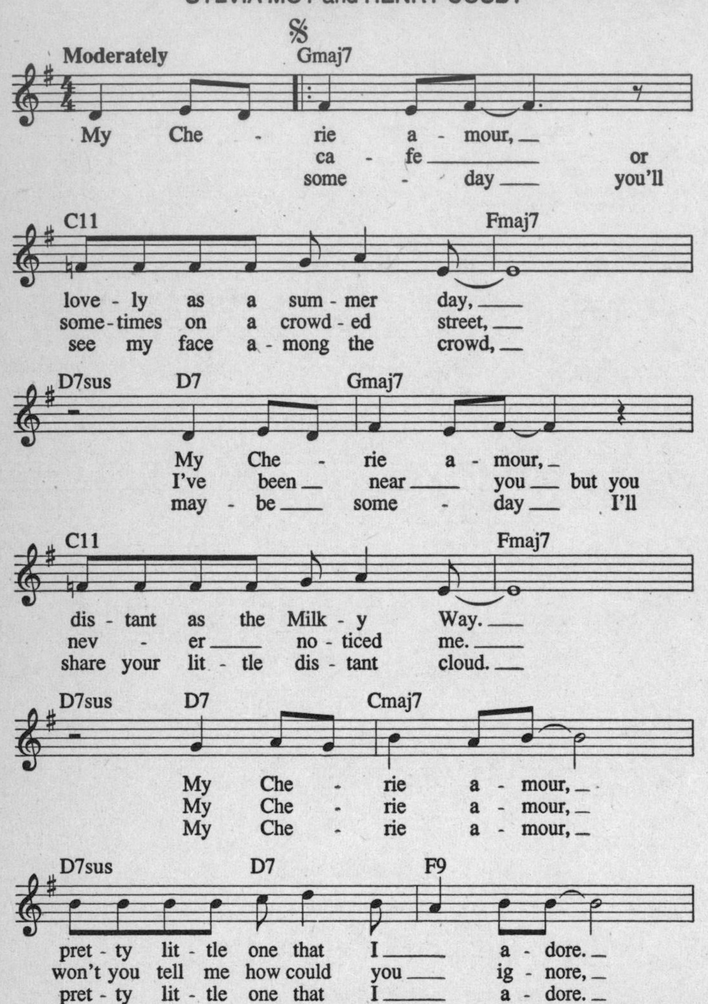

E7
A7
You're the on - ly girl my heart beats for,
that be - hind that lit - tle smile I wore,
You're the on - ly girl my heart beats for,
D7
1
G6
how I wish that you were mine.
D7#5
2, 3
Gmaj7
To Coda
N.C.
In a
La la
Cmaj7
C6
C
Fmaj7
F6
Fmaj7
la la la la, la la
1
Gmaj7
N.C.
la la la la. La la
2
D.S. al Coda
(take 3rd ending)
Gmaj7
D7
la. May - be
CODA
Cmaj7
C6
C
la la la
Repeat and Fade
Fmaj7
F6
Fmaj7
Gmaj7
la, la la la la la la. La la

MY GIRL

Words and Music by WILLIAM "SMOKEY" ROBINSON
and RONALD WHITE

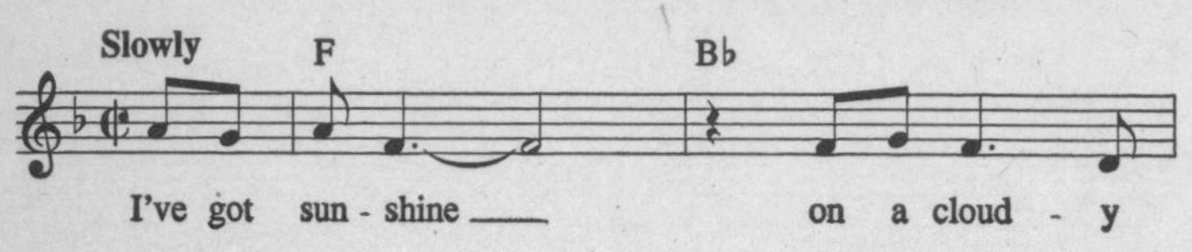
Slowly
F
Bb
I've got sun - shine ___ on a cloud - y

F
Bb
F
day; When it's cold out - side,

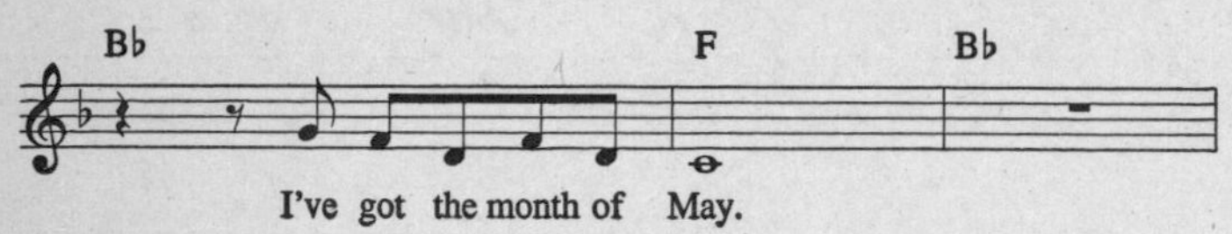
Bb
F
Bb
I've got the month of May.

F Gm Bb C F Gm
I guess you say, what can make me

Bb C F
feel this way? My girl, ___ talk-ing 'bout

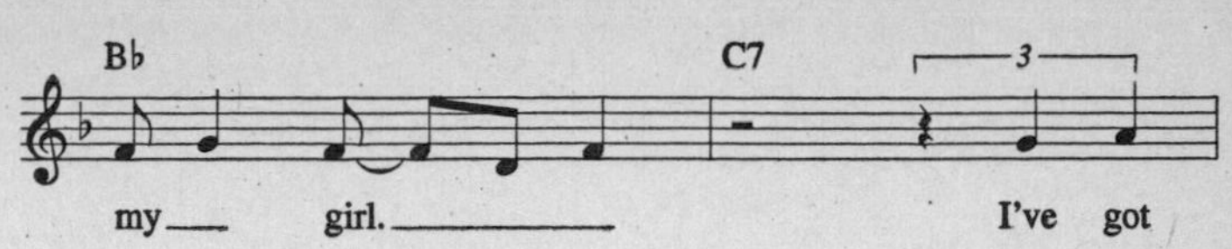
B♭
C7
3
my
girl.
I've got

F
B♭
F
so much hon-ey, the bees en-vy me;

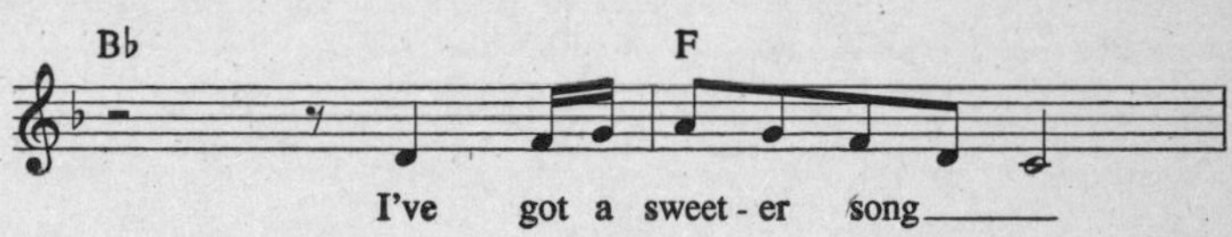
B♭
F
I've got a sweet-er song

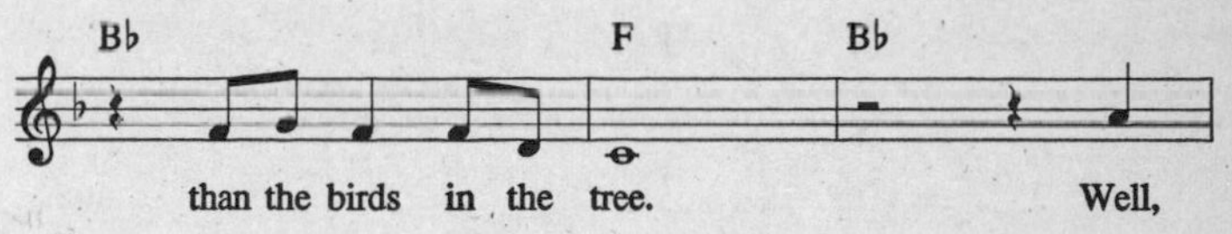
B♭
F
B♭
than the birds in the tree.
Well,

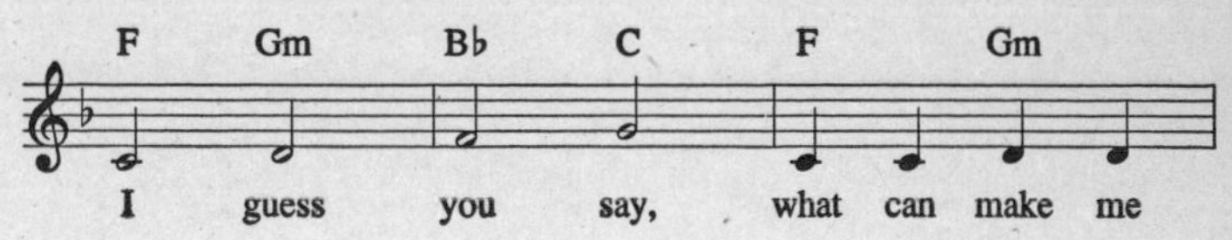
F Gm B♭ C F Gm
I guess you say, what can make me

B♭ C F
feel this way? My girl,
talk-ing 'bout

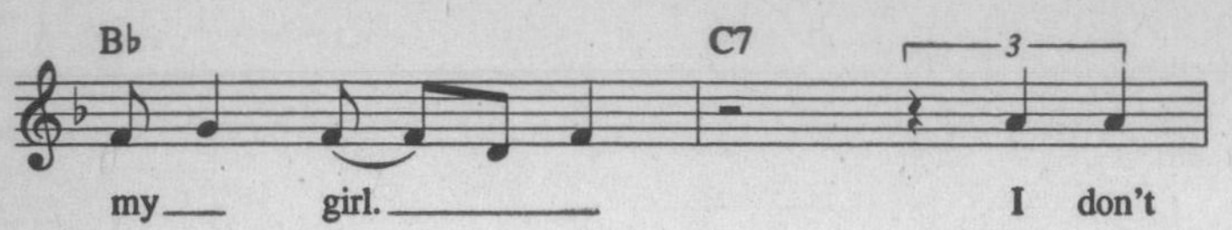
B♭
C7
3
my___ girl.___
I don't

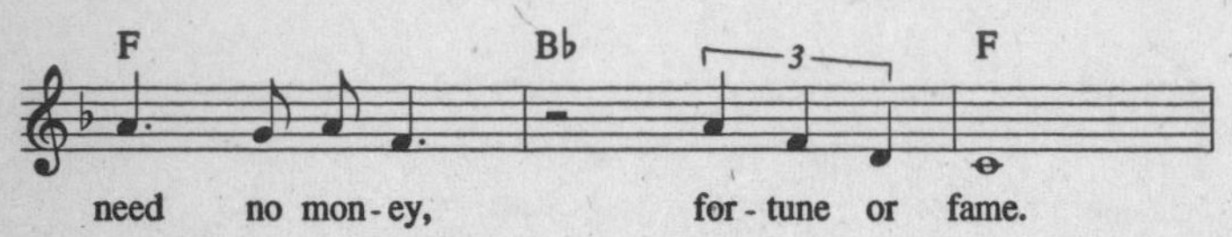
F
B♭
3
F
need no mon - ey, for - tune or fame.

B♭
3
F
I've got all the rich - es, ba - by,

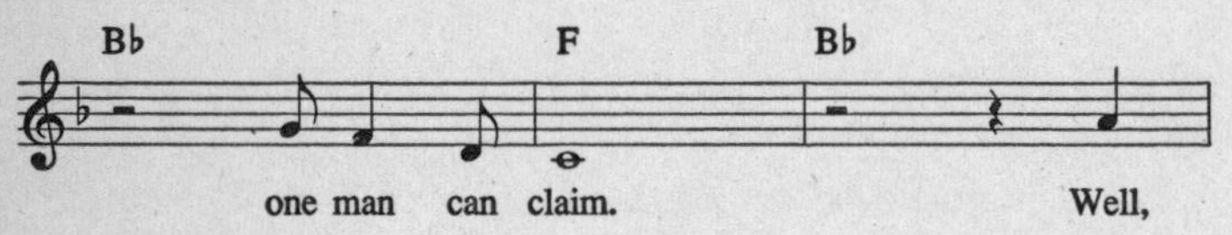
B♭
F
B♭
one man can claim.
Well,

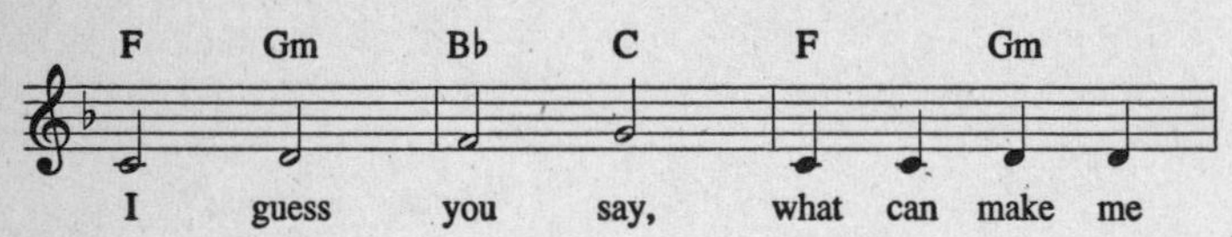
F Gm B♭ C F Gm
I guess you say, what can make me

B♭ C F
feel this way? My girl,___
talk-ing 'bout

B♭
C7
F
my girl.
I've got sun-shine on a

Gm
cloud - y day with my girl; I've

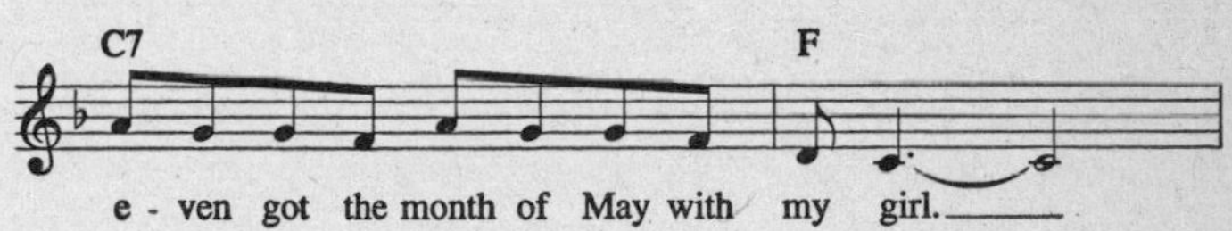
C7
F
e - ven got the month of May with my girl.

Gm
Talk-ing 'bout, talk - ing 'bout, talk - ing 'bout

C7
F
my girl. Woo! My girl.

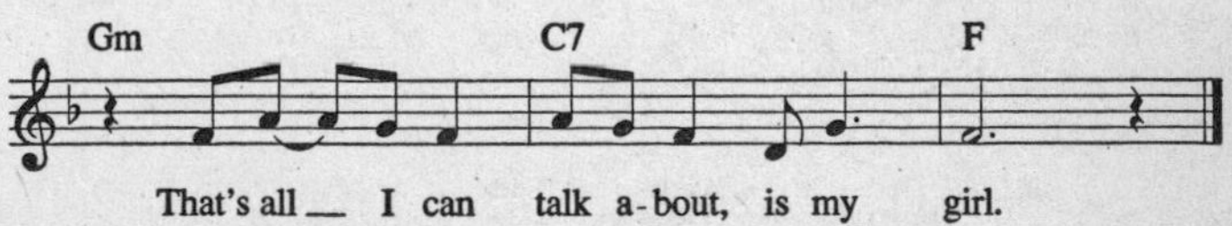
Gm
C7
F
That's all I can talk a - bout, is my girl.

MY GUY

Words and Music by
WILLIAM "SMOKEY" ROBINSON

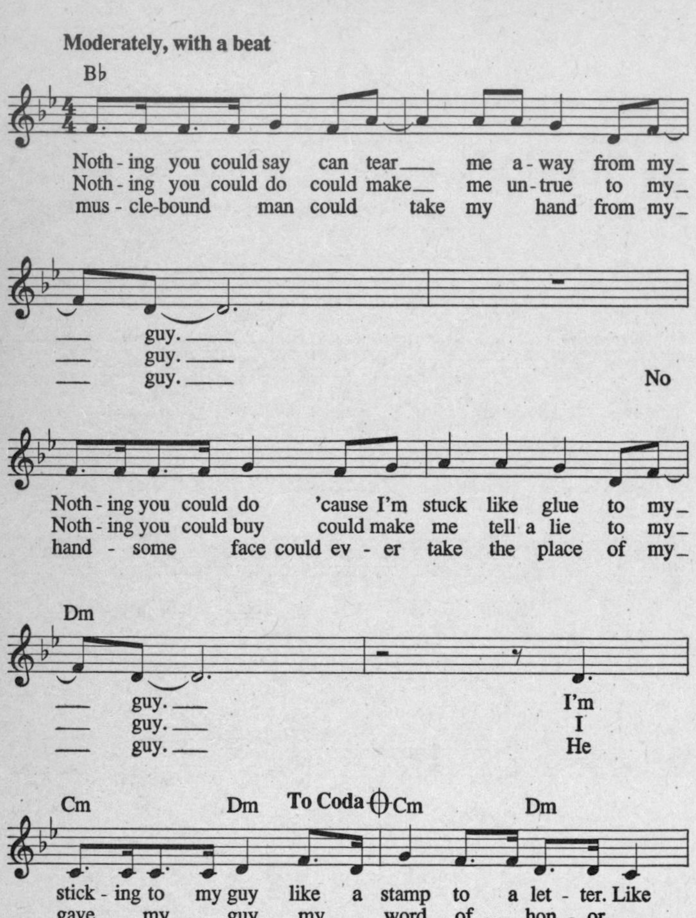
Moderately, with a beat
B♭
Noth - ing you could say can tear___ me a - way from my_
Noth - ing you could do could make__ me un - true to my_
mus - cle-bound man could take my hand from my_
___ guy. ____
___ guy. ____
___ guy. ____
No
Noth - ing you could do 'cause I'm stuck like glue to my_
Noth - ing you could buy could make me tell a lie to my_
hand - some face could ev - er take the place of my_
Dm
___ guy. ___
___ guy. ___
___ guy. ___
I'm
I
He
Cm
Dm
To Coda
Cm
Dm
stick - ing to my guy like a stamp to a let - ter. Like
gave my guy my ___ word of ___ hon - or. ___
may not be a ______

Cm
Dm
Cm
birds of a feath - er, we stick to-geth - er. I can
To be faith - ful and I'm gon - na. You

B♭
Dm
Cm
F7
tell you from the start I can't be torn a-part from my
best be be - liev-ing, I won't be de - ceiv - ing my

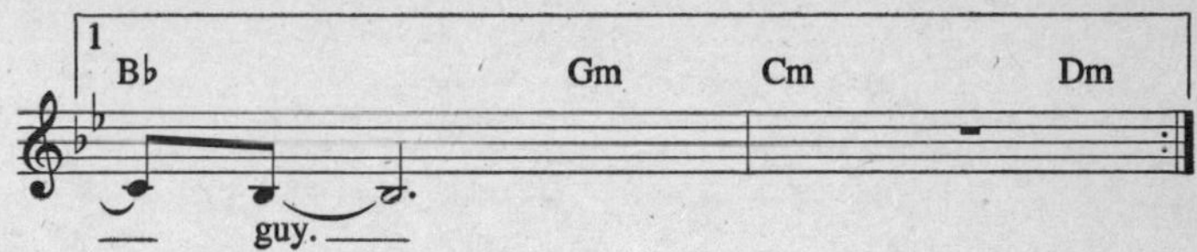
1
B♭
Gm
Cm
Dm
guy.

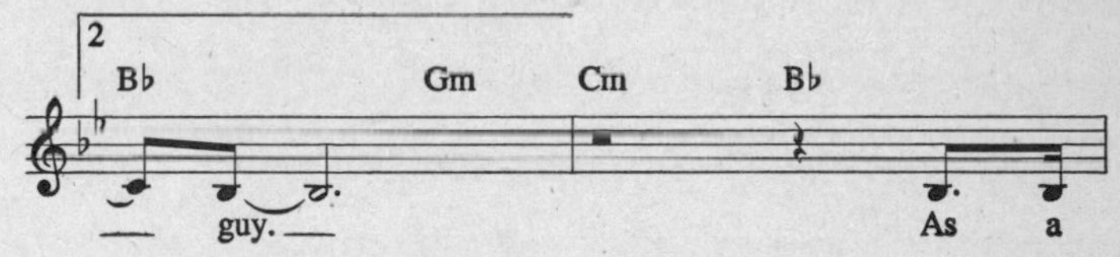
2
B♭
Gm
Cm
B♭
guy.
As a

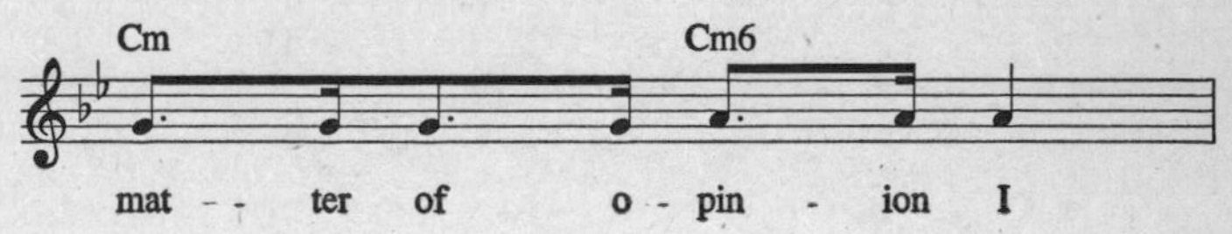
Cm
Cm6
mat - ter of o - pin - ion I

Cm
Cm6
Cm
Cm6
think he's tops.
My o-pin - ion is he's the

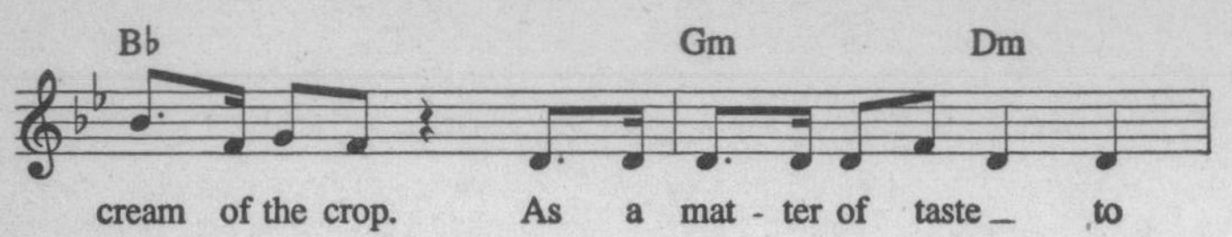
B♭
Gm
Dm
cream of the crop. As a mat - ter of taste _ to

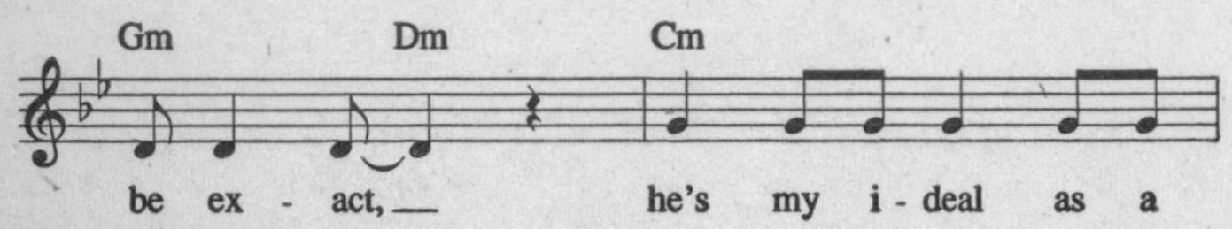
Gm
Dm
Cm
be ex - act, __ he's my i - deal as a

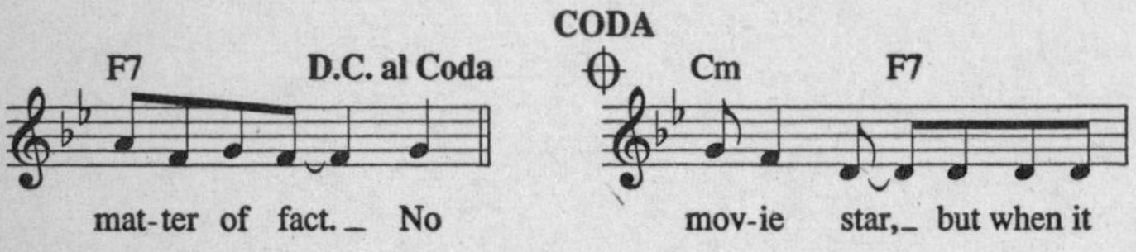
F7
D.C. al Coda
CODA
Cm
F7
mat-ter of fact. _ No
mov-ie star, _ but when it

Cm
F7
Cm
comes to be - ing hap - py we are. _ There's not a

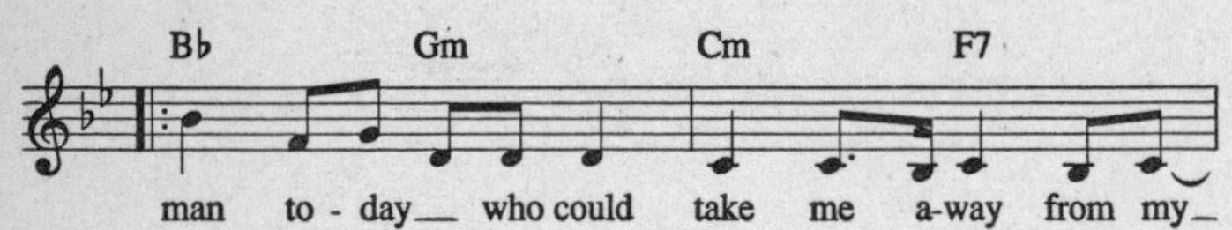
B♭
Gm
Cm
F7
man to - day __ who could take me a-way from my _

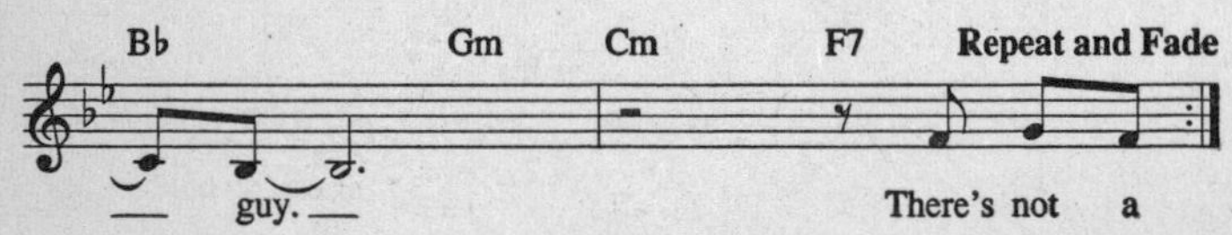
B♭
Gm
Cm
F7
Repeat and Fade
__ guy. __ There's not a

PAPA WAS A ROLLIN' STONE

Words and Music by NORMAN WHITFIELD and BARRETT STRONG

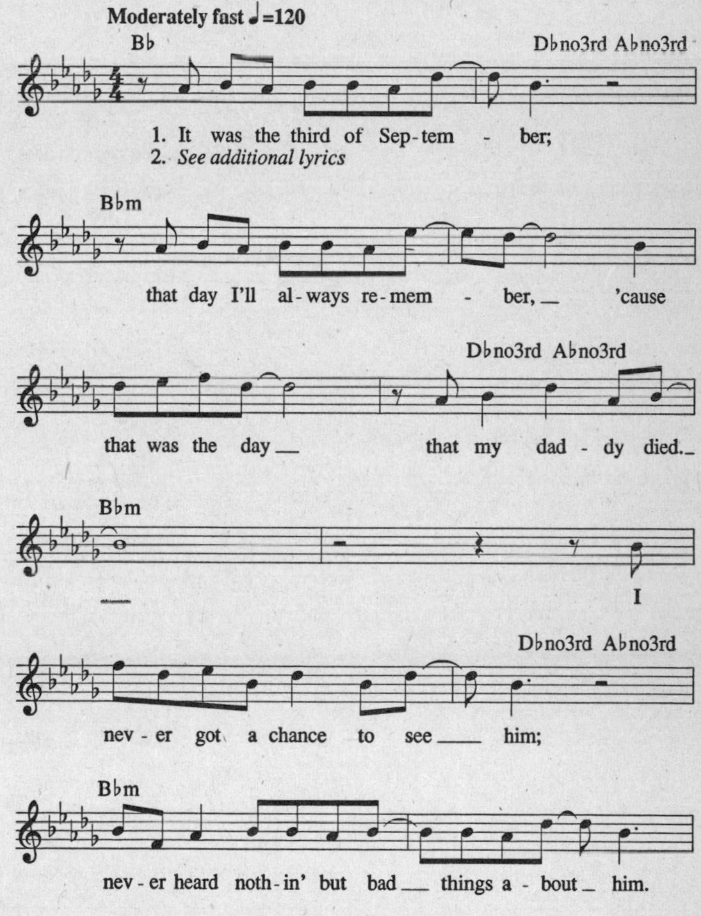
Moderately fast ♩=120
B♭
D♭no3rd A♭no3rd
1. It was the third of Sep-tem - ber;
2. See additional lyrics
B♭m
that day I'll al-ways re-mem - ber, 'cause
D♭no3rd A♭no3rd
that was the day that my dad - dy died.
B♭m
I
D♭no3rd A♭no3rd
nev - er got a chance to see him;
B♭m
nev - er heard noth-in' but bad things a - bout him.

Ma - ma I'm de - pend - ing on you

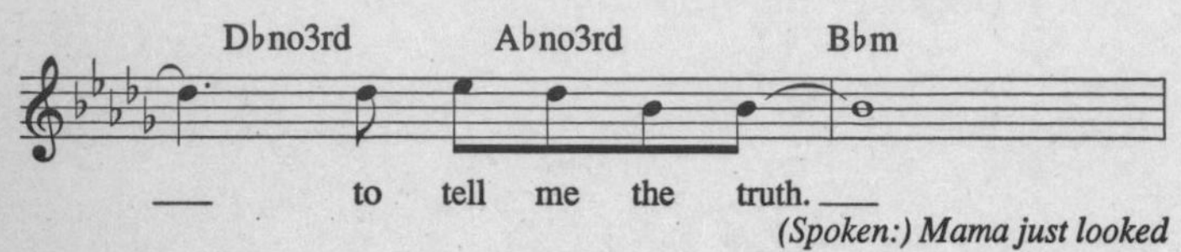
D♭no3rd
A♭no3rd
B♭m
to tell me the truth.
(Spoken:) Mama just looked

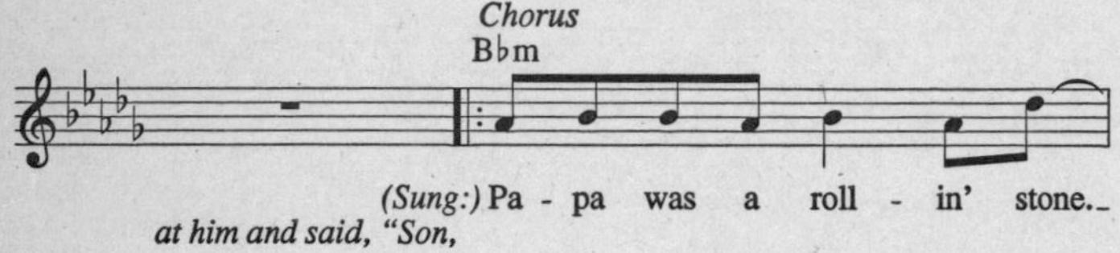
Chorus
B♭m
(Sung:) Pa - pa was a roll - in' stone.
at him and said, "Son,

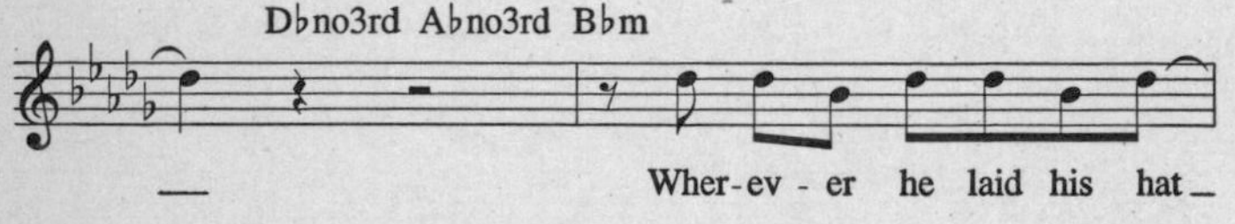
D♭no3rd A♭no3rd B♭m
Wher-ev - er he laid his hat

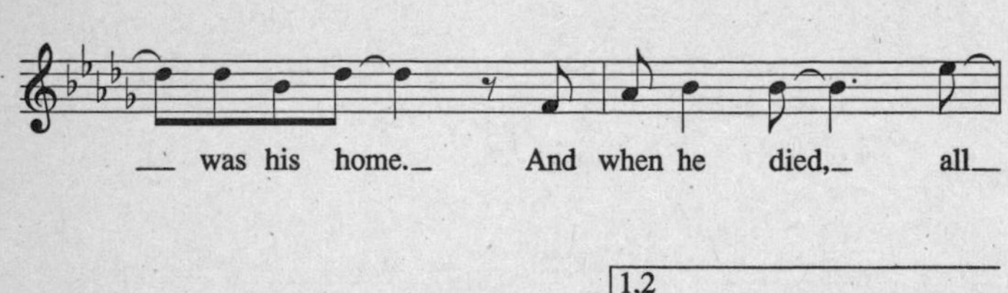
was his home. And when he died, all

D♭no3rd
A♭no3rd
1,2
B♭m
he left us was a - lone."

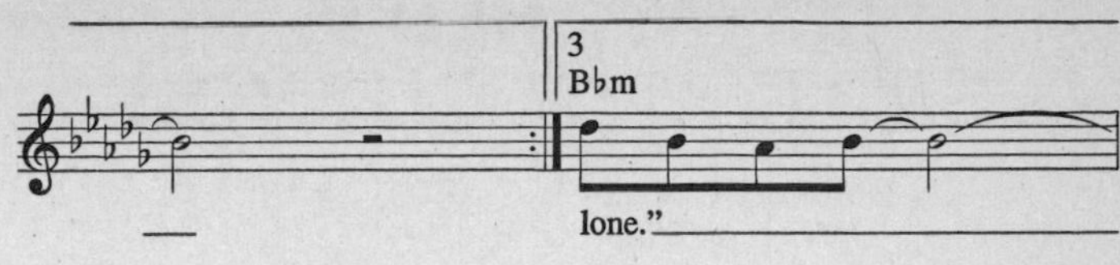

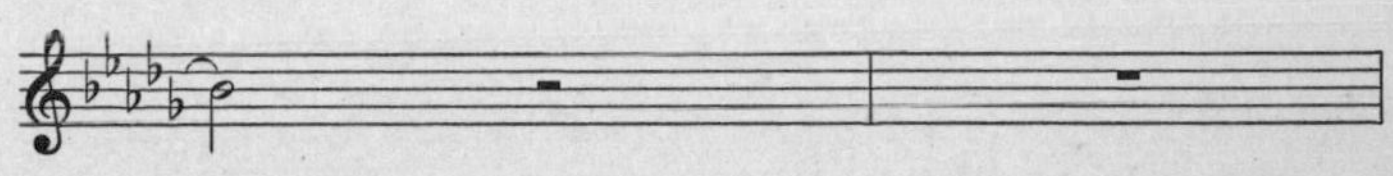

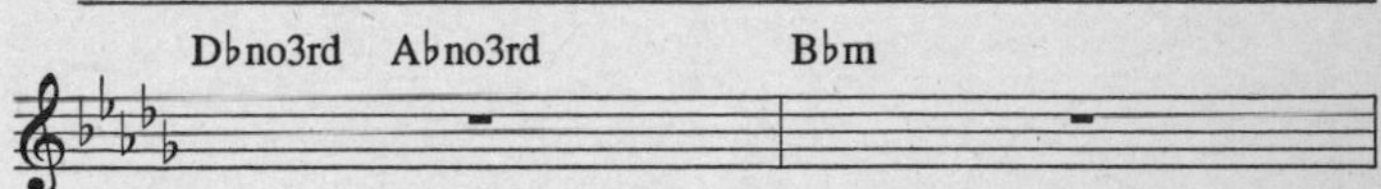

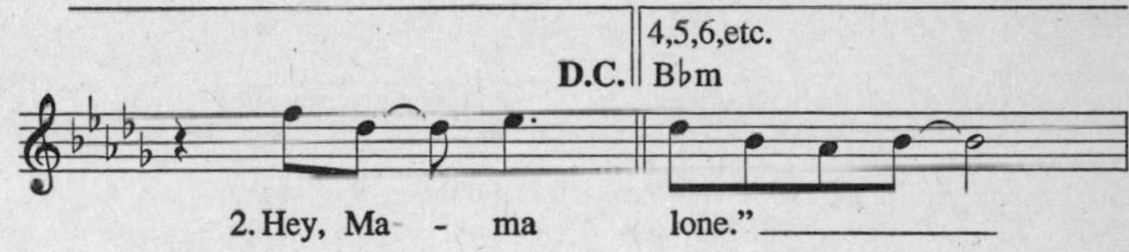

Additional Lyrics

2. Hey, Mama, I heard Papa call himself a jack of all trades.
Tell me, is that what sent Papa to an early grave?
Folks say Papa would beg, borrow or steal to pay his bills.
Hey, Mama, folks say Papa was never much on thinkin';
Spend most of his time chasin' women and drinkin'!
Mama, I'm depending on you to tell me the truth.
(Spoken:) Mama just hung her head and said, "Son,...
Chorus:

MY WORLD IS EMPTY WITHOUT YOU

Words and Music by EDWARD HOLLAND, LAMONT DOZIER and BRIAN HOLLAND

Am

I find it hard ___ for me ___ to car -
But from this lone - li - ness ___ there's ___

Em Am7 Bm G

- ry on. ___ I need your strength, ___
___ no hid - ing place. ___ In - side this cold ___

D

___ I need your ten - der touch, ___
___ and emp - ty house ___ I dwell, ___

Am

I need the love, ___ my dear, ___ I ___
in dark-ness with mem - o - ries I ___

Em Am7 D7

___ miss so ___ much. ___
___ know so ___ well. ___

Em C

(Instrumental)

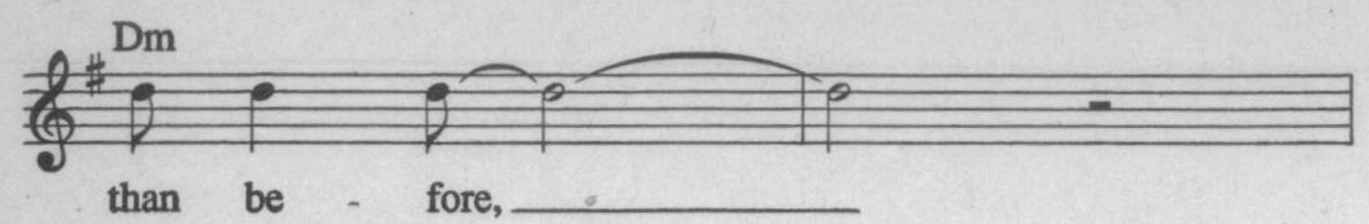
Dm
than be - fore,

B♭
I can hard - ly car - ry on

Gm
D
an - y - more.

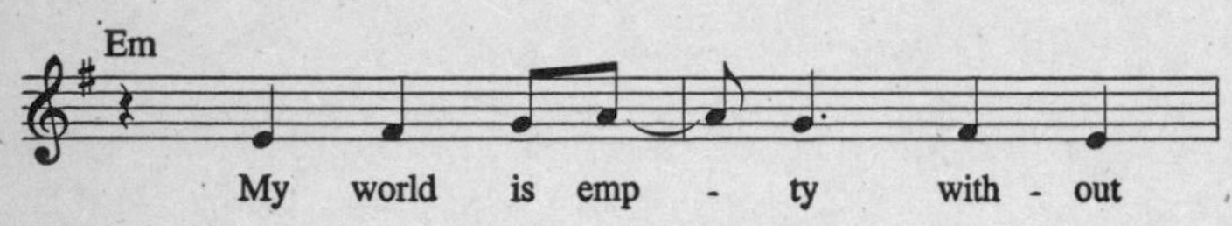
Em
My world is emp - ty with - out

C
Em
you, babe, with - out you, babe,

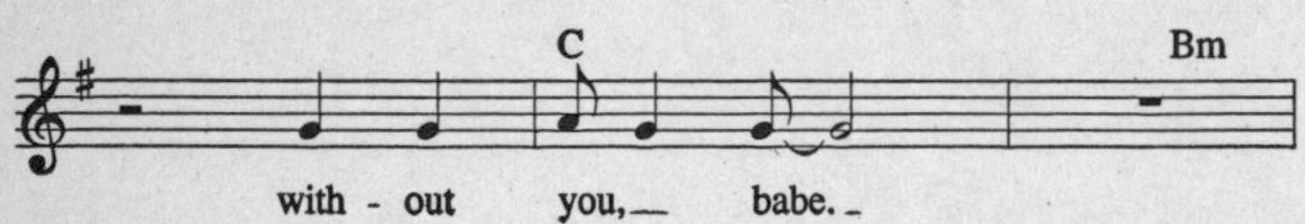
C
Bm
with - out you, babe.

G
My mind and soul have felt

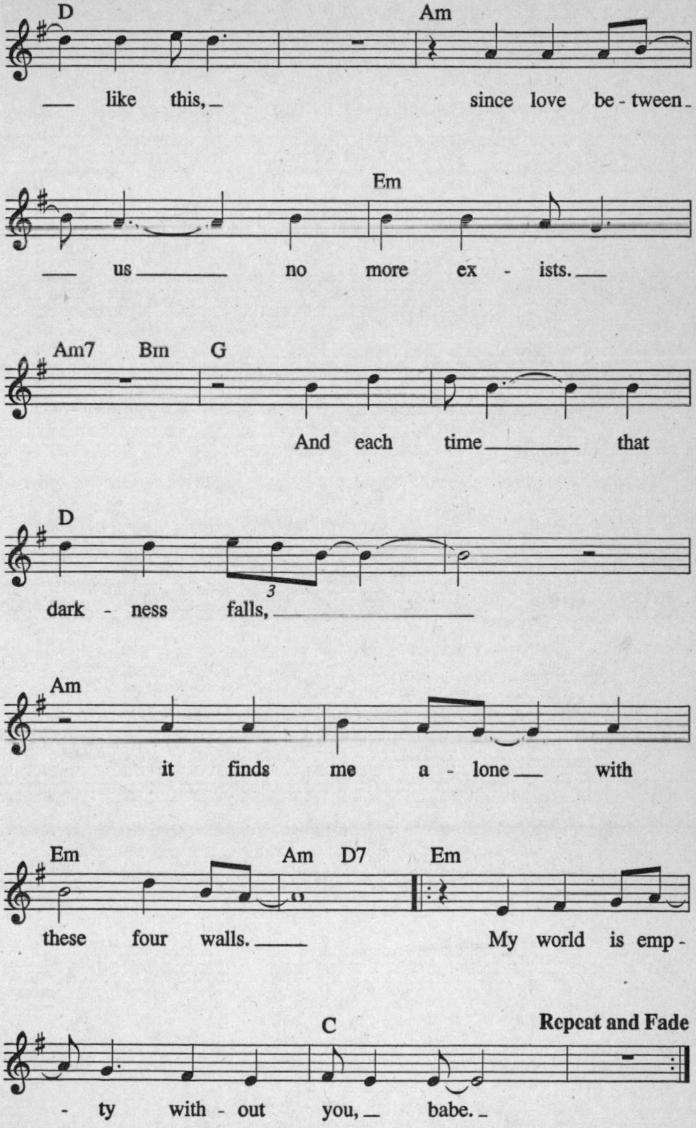

D Am

— like this, — since love be - tween —

Em

— us — no more ex - ists. —

Am7 Bm G

And each time — that

D

dark - ness falls, —

3

Am

it finds me a - lone — with

Em Am D7 Em

these four walls. — My world is emp -

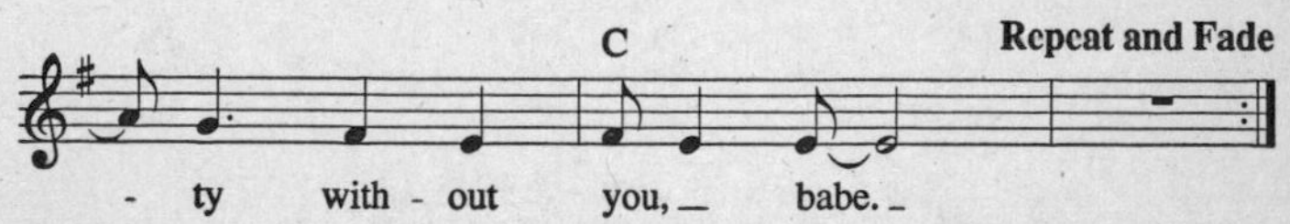

NEVER CAN SAY GOODBYE

Words and Music by
CLIFTON DAVIS

Moderately
Gmaj7
A11
Nev-er can say good-bye, No, no, no, no, I
Gmaj7
A11
nev-er can say good-bye. E - ven / Ev - 'ry
Dmaj7
tho' the pain and heart - ache seem to
time I think I've had e - nough and start
think - in' that our prob - lems soon are
Am7
fol - low me wher - ev - er I go, tho' I
head - ing for the door, there's
all gon - na work out but there's that
Dmaj7
tried and tried to hide my feel - ings, they
ver - y strange vi - bra - tions pierc - ing
same un - hap - py feel - in', there's that
Am7
al - ways seem to show. Then you
me right to the core. It says
an - guish there's that doubt. It's that

Dmaj7
try to say you're leav - ing me, and I
turn a - round, you fool, you know ___ you
same old diz - zy hang up, can't ___ do
Am7
al ways have to say no, ___
love her more and more, _
with you or with - out, ___
Tell me
1
Gmaj7 F♯m7 Em7 A11
why is it so. But I ___
2
Gmaj7 F♯m7
why is it
Em7 A11
so, don't wan-na let you
D
go. I nev-er can say good -
Dm7 (Fade with this phrase)
bye, girl, don't wan-na let you
E7 Eb
go. I nev-er can say good-
D A11
bye, no, no, no, _ no, no, no, _
1
D
I nev-er can say good-
2
Gmaj7
nev-er can say good - bye,
A11
No, no, no, no, I
Gmaj7
nev- er can say good - bye.
A11 D.S. (2nd ending till Fade)
I keep

NOWHERE TO RUN

Words and Music by LAMONT DOZIER,
BRIAN HOLLAND and EDWARD HOLLAND

Steadily
Ab Ebm Db Ab
No-where to run to, ba-by, no-where to hide.
Ebm Db Ab Ebm Db
Got no-where to run to, ba-by,
Ab Ebm Db Ab
no-where to hide. It's not love I'm a-

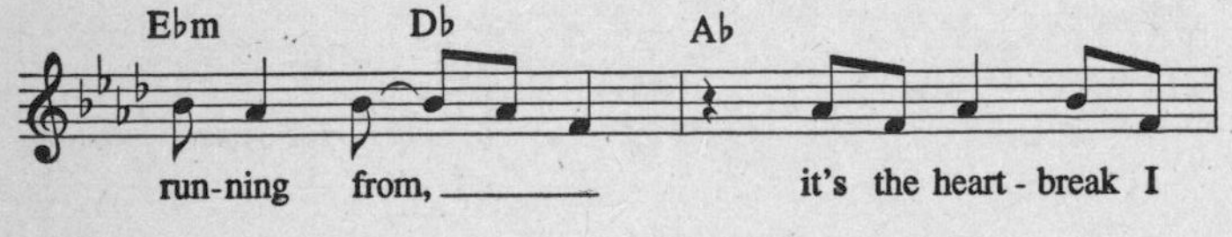
Ebm Db Ab
run-ning from, it's the heart-break I

Ebm Db Ab Ebm Db
know will come. 'Cause I know you're no good for me,

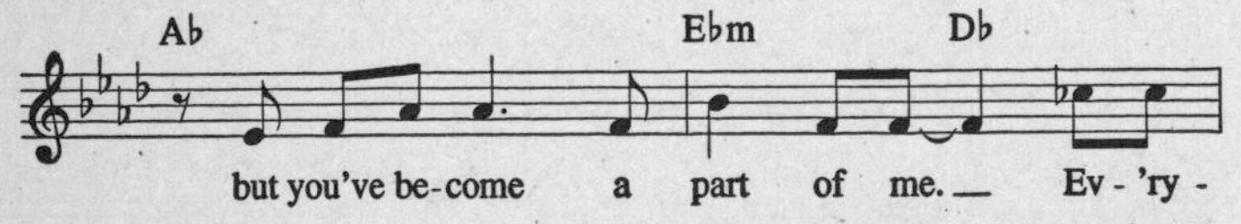
Ab Ebm Db
but you've be-come a part of me. Ev-'ry-

Ab
where I go your face I see, ev - 'ry
Ab
step I take you take with me.
No-where to run
No-where to run,
Ebm Db Ab Ebm Db
to ba - by, no-where to hide.
no - where to hide from you, ba - by.
Ab Ebm Db Ab
Got no-where to run to, ba - by, no-where to hide.
Got no-where to run to, ba - by, no-where to hide.
Ebm Db Bb7
1.,3. I know you're no good for me,
2. I know you're no good for me,
Eb7
To Coda
1
Ab
but free of you I'll nev - er be, no. Each night
but you've be-come a part of me,
Ebm Db Ab Ebm Db
as I sleep, in - to my heart you creep.

Ab Ebm Db
I wake up feel-in' sor-ry I met_ you,
Ab Ebm Db
hop-ing soon_ that I'll for-get you. When I
Ab
look in the mir-ror to comb my hair_
2
Ab
I see your face just a-smil-ing there. How can I fight_
Ebm Db Ab
_ a lov-er that should-n't be_
Ebm Db Ab Ebm Db
_ when it's so deep, so_ deep,_
Ab Ebm Db
deep in-side of me._ My love

Ab
reach-es so high I can't get o-ver it.
It's so wide I can't get a-round it, no
Ebm Db
no-where to run, no-where to hide
Ab Ebm Db Ab
from you, ba - by. Just can't get a -
D.S. al Coda
Ebm Db Ab Ebm Db
way from you, ba - by, no mat-ter how I try.
CODA
Ab Ebm Db Ab
No-where to run, no-where to hide
Ebm Db Ab Ebm Db
got No-where to run to, ba - by.

OOO BABY BABY

Words and Music by WILLIAM "SMOKEY" ROBINSON
and WARREN MOORE

Gmaj7
Am7
ba - by ba - by. Ooo,
Gmaj7
To Coda
ba - by ba - by, I'm just a -
Bm7
D11
bout at the end of my rope. But I can't stop
Bm7
D11
try-in', I can't give up hope 'cause I feel
G
Am7
some-day I'll hold you near. Whis-per I still
Bm7
Am7
D.S. al Coda
love you un-til that day is here. Ooo, I'm
CODA
Am7
Gmaj9
ba - by. Ooo.

A PLACE IN THE SUN

Words and Music by RONALD MILLER
and BRYAN WELLS

C
in' on. 'Cause there's a

Dm7 G7 C
place in the sun where there's hope for ev - 'ry -

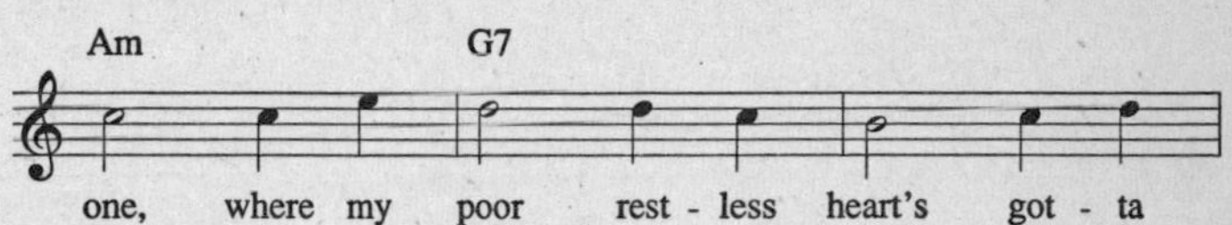
Am G7
one, where my poor rest - less heart's got - ta

C Dm7
run. There's a place in the

G7 C Am
sun and be - fore my life is done, got to

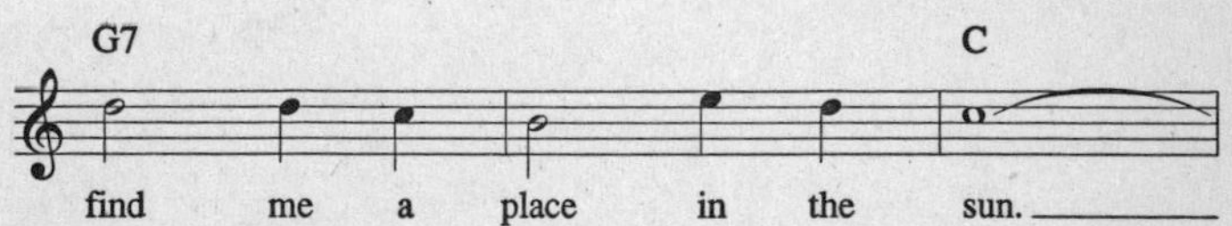
G7 C
find me a place in the sun.

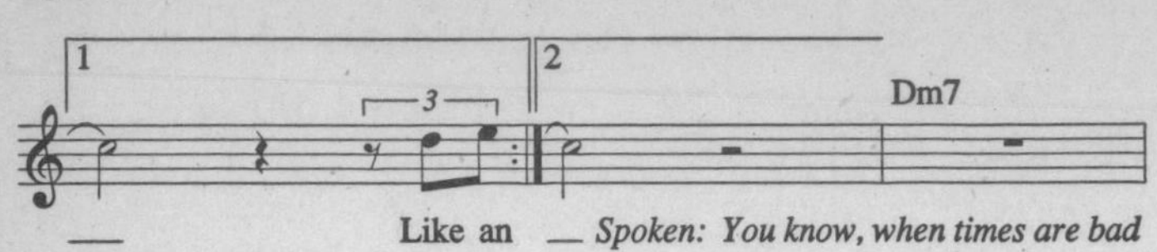
1
2
Dm7
Like an
Spoken: You know, when times are bad

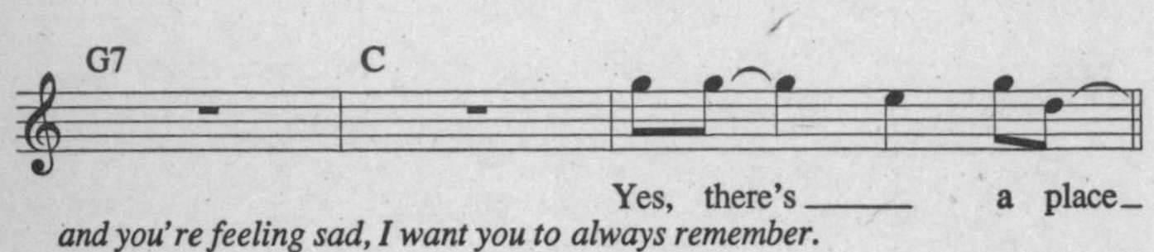
G7
C
Yes, there's a place
and you're feeling sad, I want you to always remember.

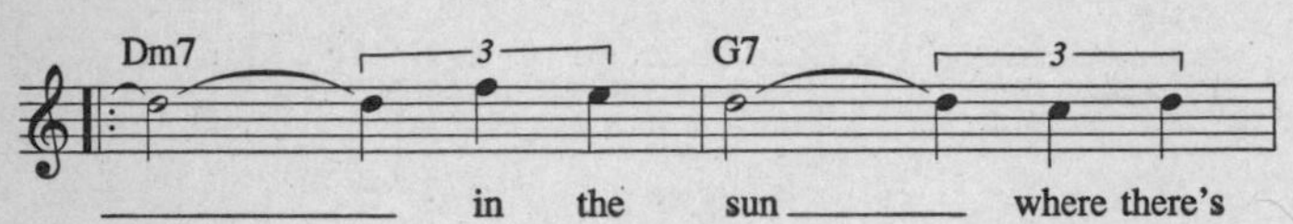
Dm7
G7
in the sun where there's

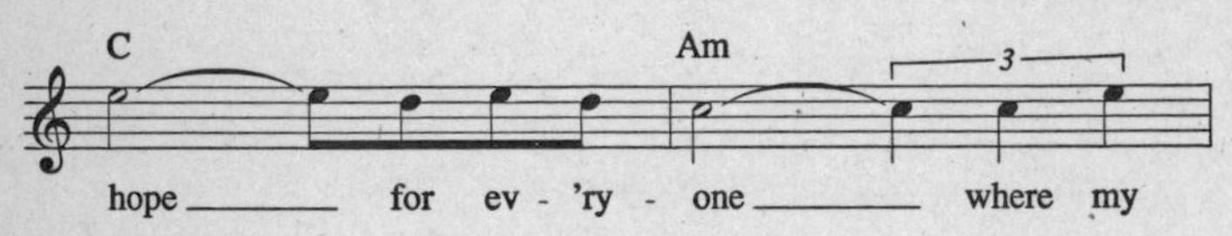
C
Am
hope for ev - 'ry - one where my

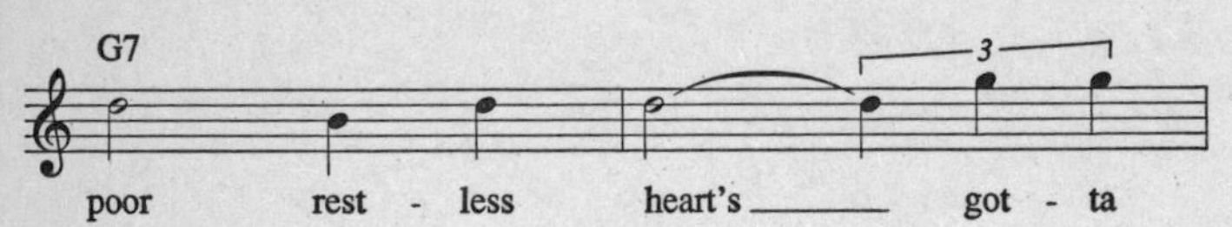
G7
poor rest - less heart's got - ta

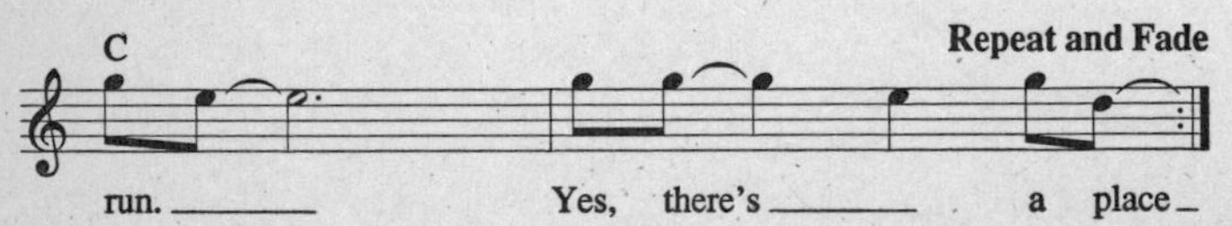
C
Repeat and Fade
run. Yes, there's a place

REACH OUT, I'LL BE THERE

Words and Music by BRIAN HOLLAND,
LAMONT DOZIER and EDWARD HOLLAND

Moderately
Am7
D
Now if you feel that you can't go on
lost and a - bout to give up
tell the way you hang your head,
be - cause all of your hope is gone,
'cause your best just ain't good e - nough
you're with - out love and now you're a - fraid
and your life
and you feel
and through your
is filled with much con - fu - sion un - til
the world has grown cold, and you're
tears you look a - round, but there's no
hap - pi - ness is just an il - lu -
drift - ing out all on your own,
peace of mind to be found,

D
- sion, and your world
and you need
(Spoken) I know what
Am7
D
a - round is crum - bl - in' down;
a hand to hold;
you're thinkin', you're alone now, no love of
G/B
dar - ling, reach out
dar - ling, reach out
your own, but dar - ling, reach out
G
B/D#
reach out,
reach out,
reach out,
D7/F#
G
B
I'll be there,
I'll be there,
Just look over your shoulder I'll be there,
Em/B
Em
with a love that will shel - ter you.
to love and com - fort you,
to give you all the love you need,

B
3
I'll be there,
and I'll be there,
and I'll be there,
Em/B
Em
with a love that will see you through.
to cher - ish and care for you.
you can al - ways de - pend on me.
B
3
1
When you feel
2
B
I'll be there
I'll be there
Em/B
Em
to al - ways see you
to love and com - fort
1
B
2
B
D.S. and Fade
through.
you.
I can

REACH OUT AND TOUCH
(Somebody's Hand)

Words and Music by NICKOLAS ASHFORD
and VALERIE SIMPSON

Moderate Waltz (easy flowing)
G7 Cmaj7
Reach out and touch some - bod - y's hand,
Am7 Dm7 G7 C
make this world a bet- ter place if you can.
Am7 G7 Cmaj7
Reach out and touch some - bod - y's hand,
Am7 Dm7 G7
make this world a bet - ter place if you
Em7 Am7 Cmaj7
can. (Just try) Take a lit - tle time out of your
If you see an old friend
3
F F+ F6
bus - y day, to give en - cour- age-ment to
on the street and he's down, re - mem - ber, his

Dm7/G Em 3 Em7 Am7
some - one who's lost the way. _ (Just try) Or
shoes could fit your _ feet. _ Just try a
Cmaj7 F F+
would I be talk - ing to a stone if I asked
lit - tle kind - ness and you'll see it's something that
F6 Dm7/G Gm7
you to share a prob - lem that's not your own.
comes ver - y nat - ur - al - ly.
A7 C7 F
We can change _ things
We can change _ things
Am Dm7 1 G9
if we start giv - ing. Why don't you
if we start giv - ing.
Am7 2 G9 Am7
reach out and Why don't you (Why don't you)
Dm7/G Cmaj7
reach out and touch some - bod - y's hand.

RIBBON IN THE SKY

Words and Music by
STEVIE WONDER

Slowly, with expression

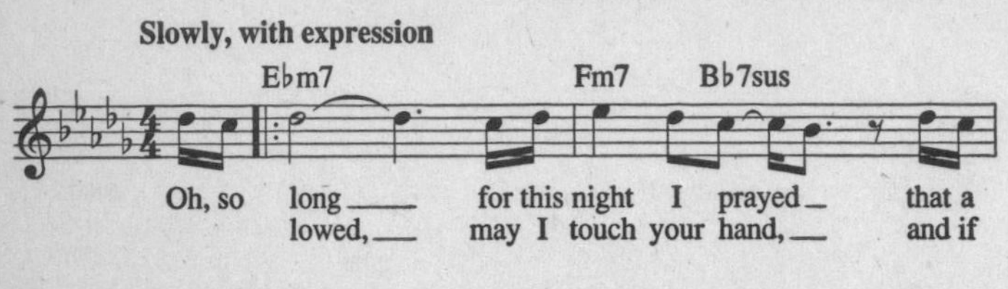

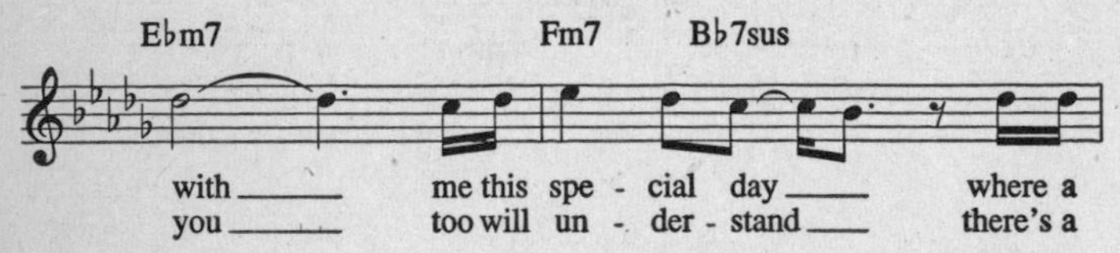

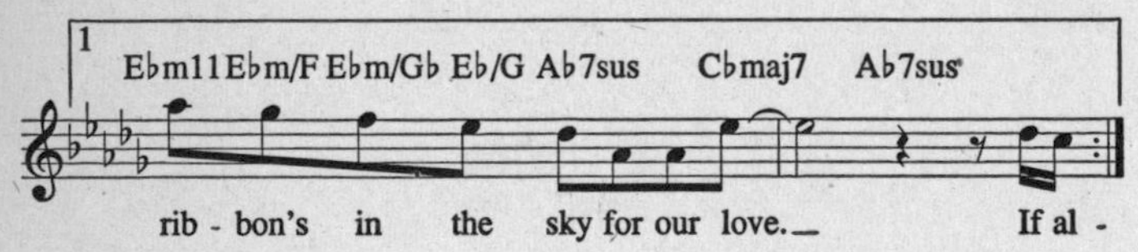

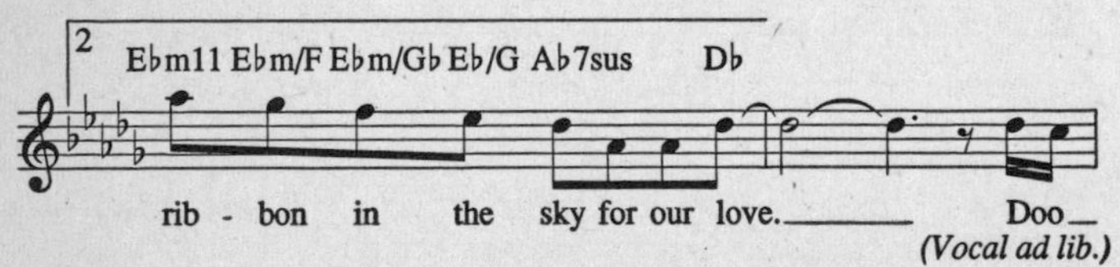

Ebm7 Ebm6 Fm7 Bb7sus

Ebm7 Ebm6 Ebm7
doo doo

Fm7 Bb7sus Ebm7 Ebm6 Ebm7
doo doo

Fm7 Bb7sus Ebm11 Ebm/F Ebm/Gb Eb/G Ab7sus Cb/A
doo doo.

A9 Em7
This is not a co -

F#m7 B7sus Em7
in - ci - dence, and far more than a

F♯m7
B7sus
Em7
luck - y chance, but what is that was

F♯m7
B7sus
Em11 Em/F♯ Em/G E/G♯ A7sus
A7sus
al - ways meant is our rib - bon in the sky for our love,

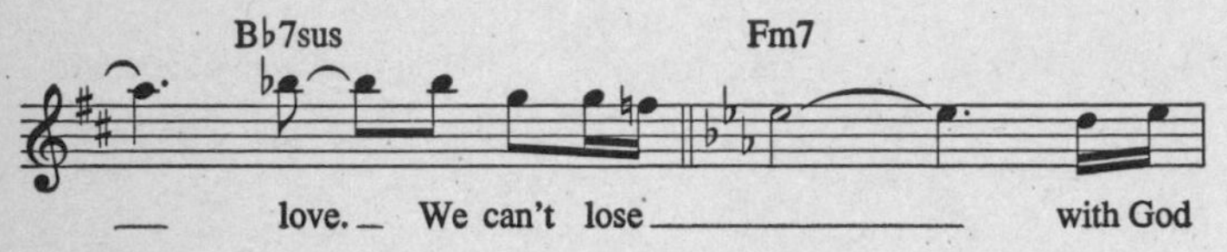
B♭7sus
Fm7
love. We can't lose with God

Gm7
C7sus
Fm7
on our side. We'll find strength in each

Gm7
C7sus
Gm7
tear we cry. From now on it will be

C7sus
Fm11 Fm/G Fm/A♭ F/A B♭7sus
you and I and our rib - bon in the sky,

Gm7♭5
C7♭9
Fm11 Fm7/G Fm7/A♭ F/A B♭7sus
Fm7
rib-bon in the sky, a rib - bon in the sky for our love.

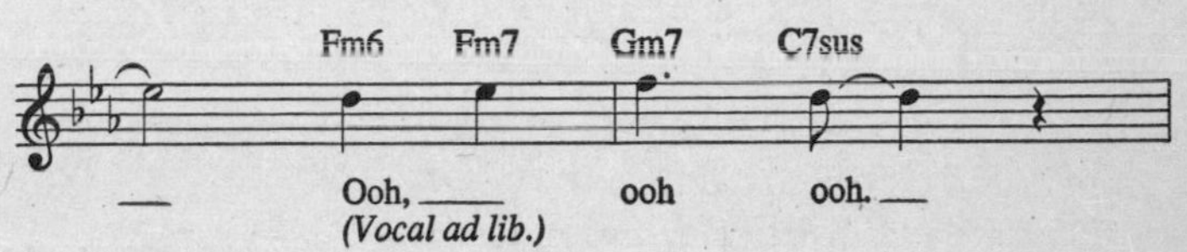
Fm6
Fm7
Gm7
C7sus
Ooh, ooh ooh.
(Vocal ad lib.)

Fm7
Fm6
Fm7
Doo doo

Gm7
C7sus
ooh

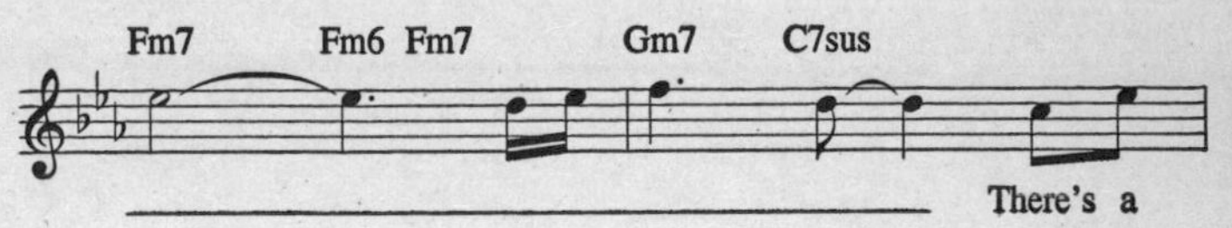
Fm7
Fm6 Fm7
Gm7
C7sus
There's a

Fm11 Fm7/G Fm7/A♭ F/A B♭7sus
E♭
rib - bon in the sky for our love.

SHAKE ME, WAKE ME

(When It's Over)

Words and Music by EDWARD HOLLAND,
LAMONT DOZIER and BRIAN HOLLAND

Gospel Rock tempo

All through this long __ and sleep - less night I hear my

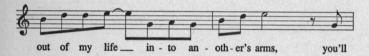

neigh - bors talk - ing ____ Say - ing that,

out of my life __ in - to an - oth - er's arms, you'll

soon be walk - ing. __ Some-bod - y shake me,

wake me when it's o - ver, __ some-bod - y

tell me that I'm dream - ing and wake me

Fmaj7
when it's o - ver.
They
Girl
Cmaj7
C7
A7
say our love ain't what it used to be and
you're what my heart de - sires, my
Dm7
Fm6
ev - 'ry - one knows but me; I
whole world you've in - spired; I can't
Cmaj7
C7
A7
close my ears not want - ing to hear but the
bear to be los - ing you 'cause I've
To Coda
Dm
Fm6
F6
words are loud and clear. Through these
loved you my whole life through. (Instrumental)
Gm7
G
walls so thin I hear my neigh - bors when they say,
"She don't love him." (She don't love him) They say my

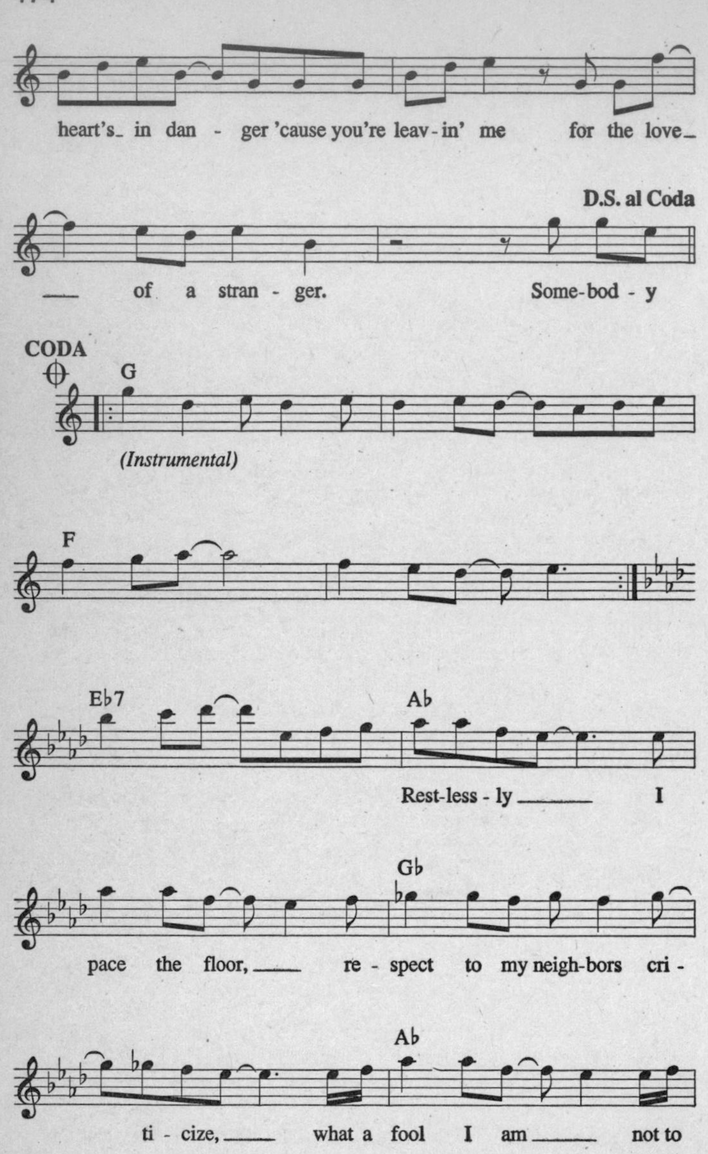
heart's_ in dan - ger 'cause you're leav - in' me for the love_
D.S. al Coda
___ of a stran - ger. Some-bod - y
CODA
G
(Instrumental)
F
Eb7
Ab
Rest-less - ly ______ I
Gb
pace the floor, ____ re - spect to my neigh-bors cri -
Ab
ti - cize, _____ what a fool I am _____ not to

Gb
re - al - ize, you don't want me by your side.
Db
Wipe the tears free from my
Bb7
Ebm7
face I can't be - lieve I've been re -
Gbm
Db
placed. If I've ev - er, ev - er dreamed be -
Db7
Bb7
Ebm
fore some-bod - y tell me I'm dream-ing now,
Gbm
Ab
and then shake me, wake me
Gb
Repeat and Fade
when it's o - ver. Some-bod - y

SHOP AROUND

Words and Music by BERRY GORDY
and WILLIAM "SMOKEY" ROBINSON

When I be-came of age my moth-er called me to her side, she said,

"Son, you're grow-ing up now, pret-ty soon you'll take a bride." And then she

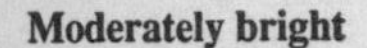

said, "Just be - cause you've be - come a young man now,
there's some things that I want you to know now.

there's still some things that you don't un - der - stand now;
Just as sure as the wind's gon - na blow now,

be - fore you ask some girl for her hand, now___
wom - en come and the wom - en gon - na go, now___

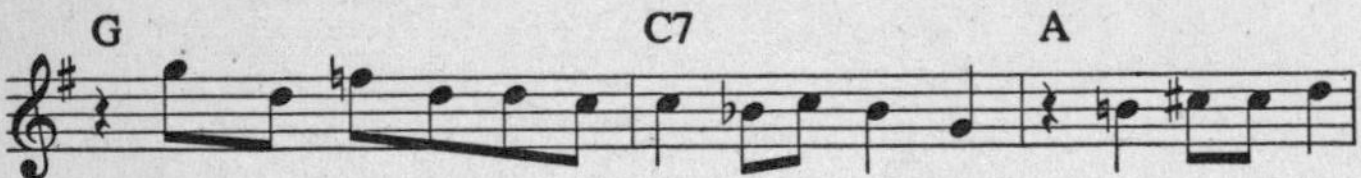

keep your free-dom for as long as you can now." }
be - fore you tell 'em that you love 'em so now." } My ma-ma told

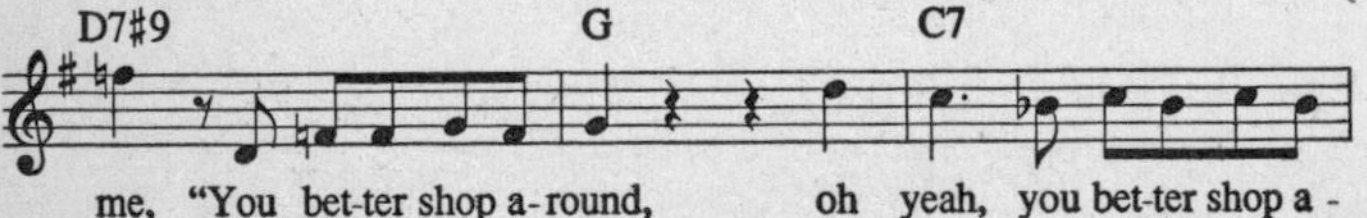

me, "You bet-ter shop a-round, oh yeah, you bet-ter shop a -

G
1
D
2
D
round." (shop, shop a-round) Ah, round)
C7
A - try to get your-self a bar - gain son.
G7
Don't be sold on the ver - y first one.
C7
A - pret - ty girls come a dime a doz - en, a -
D7
try to find one who's gon - na give you true lov - in'.
G
C7
Be - fore you take a girl and say I do now,
G7
C7
To Coda
A7
make sure she's in love with-a you now." My ma-ma told

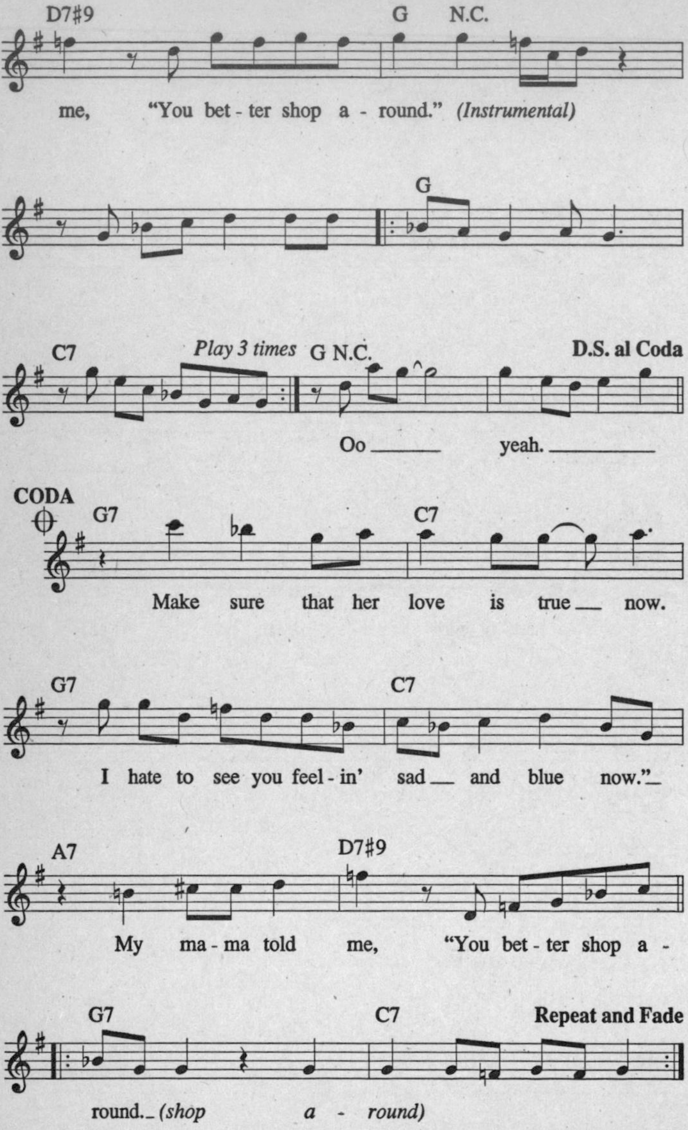

D7#9
G N.C.
me, "You bet - ter shop a - round." (Instrumental)
G
C7
Play 3 times
G N.C.
D.S. al Coda
Oo ______ yeah. ______
CODA
G7
C7
Make sure that her love is true __ now.
G7
C7
I hate to see you feel - in' sad __ and blue now."__
A7
D7#9
My ma - ma told me, "You bet - ter shop a -
G7
C7
Repeat and Fade
round._ (shop a - round)

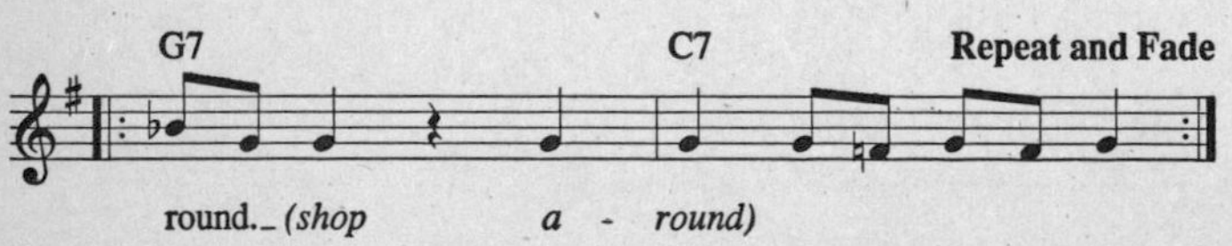

SMILING FACES SOMETIMES

Words and Music by NORMAN WHITFIELD
and BARRETT STRONG

Moderately
Em F#m7 Em F#m7♭9 Em F#m7♭9
Smil - ing fac - es some - times pre - tend to
Em F#m7 Em F#m7 Em F#m7
be your friend. Smil - ing fac - es show no trac - es
Em F#m7 Em F#m7
of the e - vil that lurks with - in.
Em F#m7 Em F#m7
Smil - ing fac - es, smil - ing fa - ces some -
Em F#m7 Em F#m7
times they don't tell the truth.
Em F#m7 Em F#m7
Smil - ing fac - es, smil - ing fac - es tell

Em
F#m7
Em
F#m7
To Coda
lies
and I got proof
The
Be -
Your
1
truth is in the eyes 'cause the eyes don't lie, a -
men.
Re - mem-ber, a smile is just a frown turned
up - side down
my friend.
So,
hear me when I'm say - ing
2
ware. Be - ware of the
hand - shake
that hides the snake.
I'm tell - in' you
be - ware of the

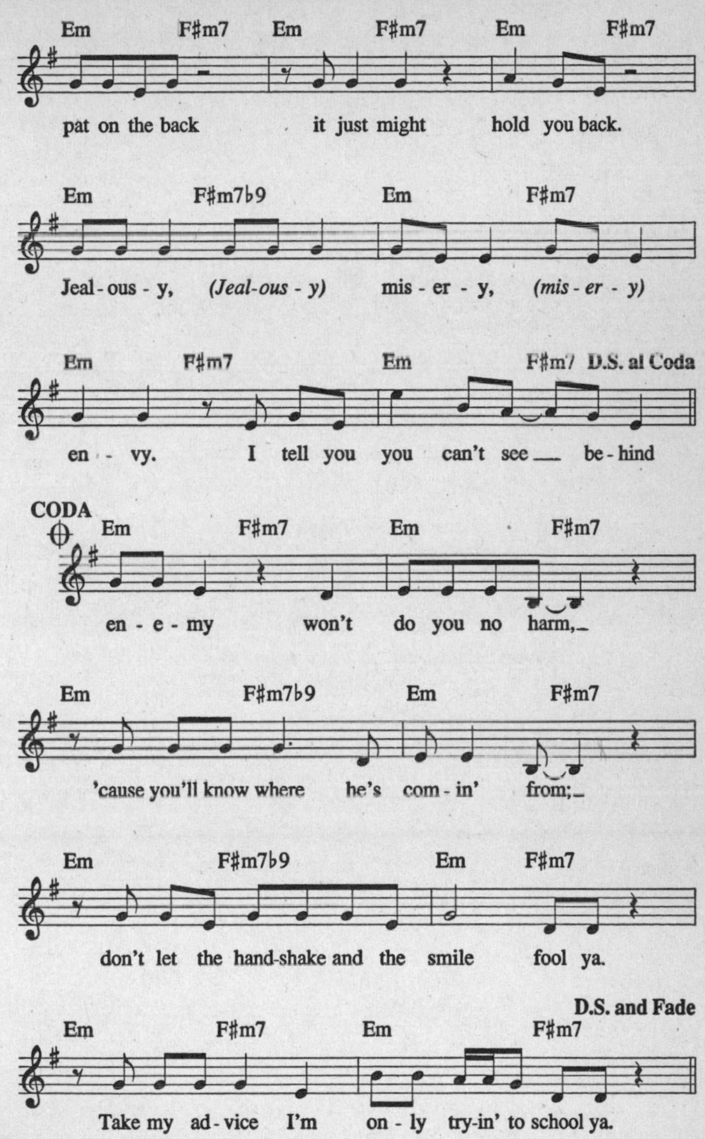
Em F#m7 Em F#m7 Em F#m7
pat on the back it just might hold you back.
Em F#m7♭9 Em F#m7
Jeal - ous - y, (Jeal-ous - y) mis - er - y, (mis - er - y)
Em F#m7 Em F#m7 D.S. al Coda
en - vy. I tell you you can't see ___ be - hind
CODA
Em F#m7 Em F#m7
en - e - my won't do you no harm, _
Em F#m7♭9 Em F#m7
'cause you'll know where he's com - in' from; _
Em F#m7♭9 Em F#m7
don't let the hand-shake and the smile fool ya.
D.S. and Fade
Em F#m7 Em F#m7
Take my ad - vice I'm on - ly try-in' to school ya.

SIGNED, SEALED, DELIVERED I'M YOURS

Words and Music by STEVIE WONDER, SYREETA WRIGHT, LEE GARRETT and LULA MAE HARDAWAY

Moderately
F
Dm
1. Like a fool I went and stayed _ too long; _
2. Then that time I went and said ___ good-bye; _
3., 4. See additional lyrics
F
Dm
F7
Now I'm won-derin' if your love's still strong. _
Now I'm back and not a-shamed to cry. ___
Oo ba -
B♭9
Gm7/C
- by, here I am, _ signed, sealed, de-liv-ered; I'm yours. _
1,3
F
2,4
F
Here I am
F7
B♭
Gm7/C
F
F7
ba - by, signed, sealed, de-liv-ered; I'm yours. _
B♭
B♭7
F
F7
B♭
Gm7
Here I am ba - by, signed, sealed, de-liv-ered; I'm yours._

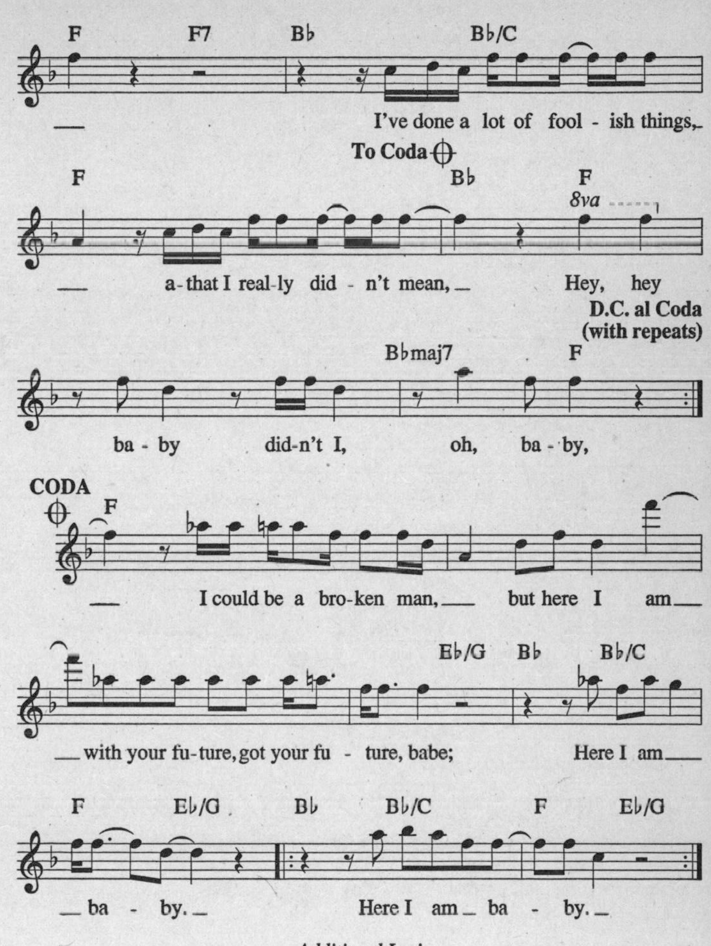

Additional Lyrics

3. Seen a lot of things in this old world,
   When I touched them they did nothing, girl.
   Oo baby, here I am signed, sealed, delivered, I'm yours.

4. Ooh-wee babe, you set my soul on fire;
   That's why I know you're my one and only desire.
   Oo baby, here I am signed, sealed, delivered, I'm yours.

SIR DUKE

Words and Music by
STEVIE WONDER

Moderately
N.C.
B
Mu - sic is a world with -
Mu - sic knows it is and
G#m
in it - self with a
al - ways will be one of
G
F#7
lan - guage we all un - der - stand,
the things that life just won't quit.
B
with an e - qual op - por -
But here are some of mu - sic's

G#m
tu - ni - ty for all to
pi - o - neers, that time will
G
sing dance and clap their hands.
not al - low us to for - get.
F#7 F7
But just be -
For there's
E9 Eb9 D9 Db9
cause a re - cord has a groove don't
Ba - sie, Mil - ler, Sach - mo, and the
D9 Eb9 E9
make it in the groove but you can
king of all, Sir Duke, and with a
Eb9 D9 Db9
tell right a - way at let - ter A when the
voice like El - la's ring - in' out there's no
D9 Eb9 E9 F9 F#9
peo - ple start to move.
way the band can lose.

B
They
You
can feel it all
Fm
o - ver.
Emaj7
They
You
can feel it all
C#m7
o - ver,
F#11
peo - ple.
B
They
You
can feel it all
Fm
o - ver.
Emaj7
They
You
can feel it all
C#m7
o - ver,
F#11
peo - ple, go!

N.C.
2nd time Fine

SOMEBODY'S WATCHING ME

Words and Music by
ROCKWELL

Moderate Dance beat

Cm Fm/A♭

1.*(Spoken:) I'm just an av-erage man, with an av-erage life.*
2., 3. *See additional lyrics*

Cm

I work from nine to five; —

A♭ B♭

hey hell, I pay the price. —

Cm

All I want is to be left a - lone —

Fm/A♭
Cm
in my av-erage home; but why do I al-ways feel

1,3
To next strain
2
Ab
Bb
Ab
Bb
D.C.
like I'm in the Twi-light Zone, and... (2.) I just par-a - noid?
3. "Psy-cho" too much That's why...

Chorus

Cm Fm/Ab

I al - ways feel like some - bod - y's watch - ing me.

Cm Ab Ab/Bb

And I have so pri - va - cy. Woh

Cm Fm/Ab

I al - ways feel like some bod y's watch - ing me.

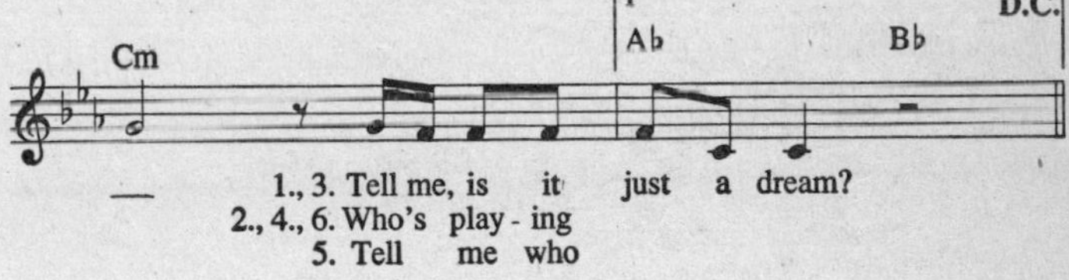
1
D.C.
Cm
Ab
Bb
1., 3. Tell me, is it just a dream?
2., 4., 6. Who's play - ing
5. Tell me who

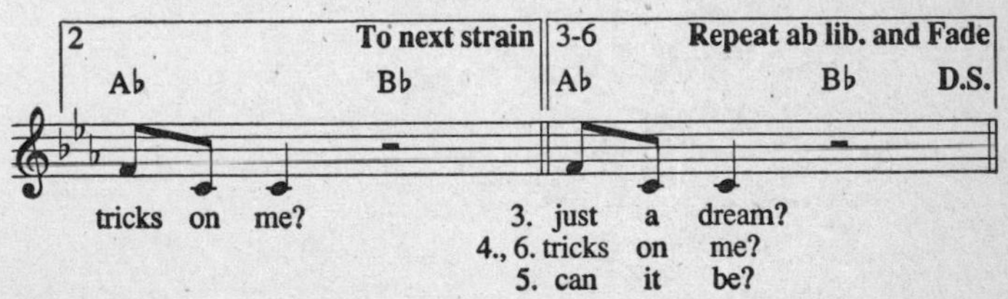
2
To next strain
3-6
Repeat ab lib. and Fade
Ab
Bb
Ab
Bb
D.S.
tricks on me?
3. just a dream?
4., 6. tricks on me?
5. can it be?

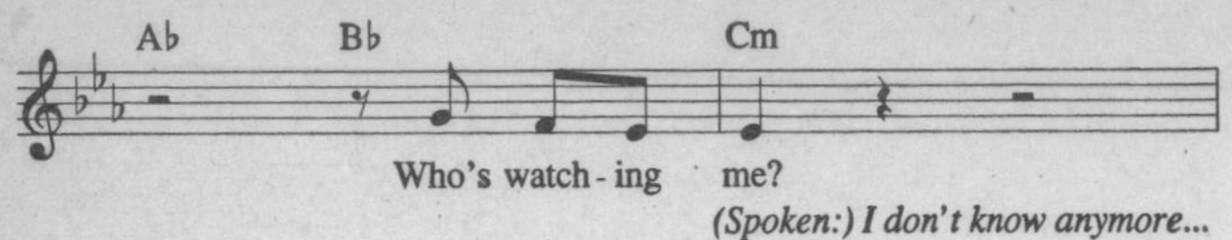
Ab
Bb
Cm
Who's watch - ing me?
(Spoken:) I don't know anymore...

Bb
Cm
Who's watch - ing?
are the neighbors watching.
Well, it's the mailman watching me;

Ab
Bb
Cm
Fm9/Ab
Tell me who's watch-ing.
and I don't feel safe anymore. Oh, what a mess. I

Cm
Ab
Ab/Bb
D.S.
3
won-der who's watch-ing me now, (WHO?) the I. R. S.?

Additional Lyrics

2. When I come home at night,
I bolt the door real tight.
People call me on the phone I'm trying to avoid.
Well, can the people on T.V. see me,
Or am I just paranoid?

3. When I'm in the shower,
I'm afraid to wash my hair,
'Cause I might open my eyes
And find someone standing there.
People say I'm crazy,
Just a little touched,
But maybe showers remind me of
"Psycho" too much.,
That's why...
To Chorus:

SOMEDAY WE'LL BE TOGETHER

Words and Music by JACKEY BEAVERS, JOHNNY BRISTOL and HARVEY FUQUA

Moderately
D
1. You're far a - way
2.,3. See additional lyrics
D7
from me my love,
G
and just as sure my, my ba - by
G♯dim
as there are stars a - bove, I wan-na say, I wan-na say, I wan-na
D
To Coda
A
say some - day we'll be to -
3
G7
D
geth - er;
(Yes we will, yes we will)

A

say some - day we'll be to -

G7 D

geth - er.

(I know, I know, I know, I know, I)

G

Long time a - go ___ my, my sweet thing, ___

___ I made a big ___ mis - take, _ hon - ey.

D

I ___ say, I ___

D7

___ said ___ good-bye. Oh, ___ Oh ___ ba -

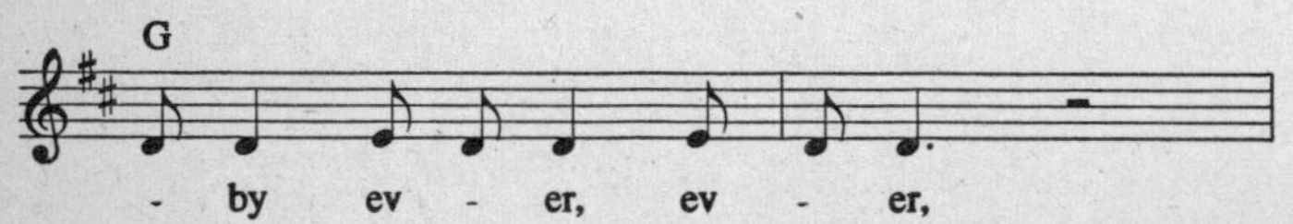

Gm
Gm6
E7
ev - er since that day now, now all

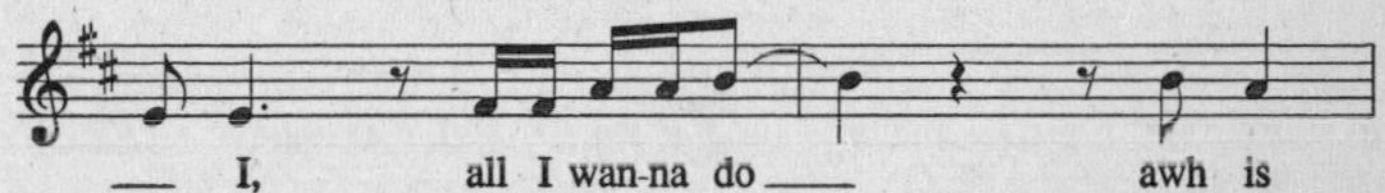
I, all I wan-na do awh is

A
D.C. al Coda
cry, cry. Oh hey, hey, hey.

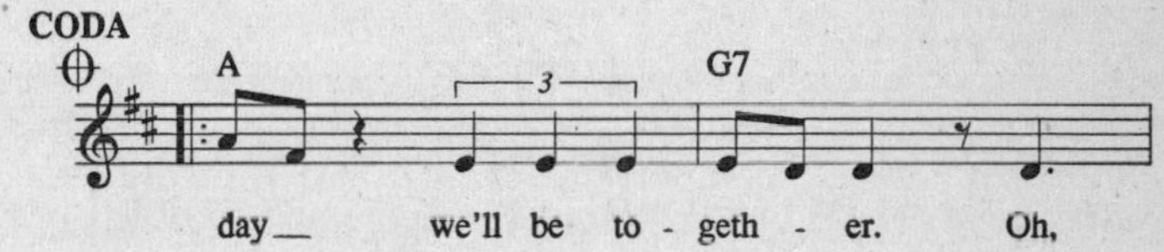
CODA
A
G7
day we'll be to - geth - er. Oh,

D
Repeat and Fade
yes we will, yes we will. Some

Additional Lyrics

2. You know my love is yours, baby
Oh, right from the start
You, you, you possess my soul now honey
And I know, I know you own my heart.
And I wanna say someday we'll be together.
Yes we will, yes we will.

3. I long for you, every night,
Just to kiss your sweet, sweet lips,
Hold you ever so tight and I wanna say
Someday we'll be together.
Oh, yes we will, yes we will.

STANDING IN THE SHADOWS OF LOVE

Words and Music by EDWARD HOLLAND, LAMONT DOZIER and BRIAN HOLLAND

Steady Rock
Am
Am/G
Stand-ing in the shad-ows of love, I'm get-ting
Stand-ing in the shad-ows of love, I'm get-ting
Fmaj7
E
E7
read-y for the heart-aches to come. Can't you see me
read-y for the heart-aches to come. Don't you see me
Am
Am/G
stand-ing in the shad-ows of love? I'm get-ting
stand-ing in the shad-ows of love? Try my best to get
Fmaj7
E
read-y for the heart-aches to come. I want to
read-y for the heart-aches to come. All a-
F
Gm
C
run but there's no-where to go 'cause
lone, I'm des-tined to be with mis-
F
Gm
C
heart-aches will fol-low me I know.
er-y my on-ly com-pan-y.

F
Gm
C
With-out your love,
the love
I need,
It may come to - day,
it might come to - mor -
F
Gm C
it's the be - gin - ning of the end
for me.
row.
But it's for sure, I ain't got noth - ing
but sor -
Dsus
Dm
'Cause you're tak - ing a - way all my rea -
- row.
Now don't your con - science kind of
- sons for liv - ing
when you
both - er you?
How can you
A
pushed a - side
all the love
I've been
watch me cry
af - ter all
I've done
B♭dim7
giv - ing.
Now wait a min - ute.
for you?
Now hold on a min - ute.
N.C.
Did - n't I treat you right
now, ba - by,
Gave you all the love
I had now

did-n't I?
did-n't I?
Did - n't I do the best_ I could,now
When you needed me I was al - ways there now
1
did - n't I? So don't you leave_ me
2
was-n't I?
Gm C
Stand-ing in the shad-ows of love,_
F Gm C
get-ting read - y for the heart-aches to come._
F Gm C
I'm try - ing not to cry out loud._
F Gm C
You know cry-ing, it ain't gon-na help me now.
Dsus Dm
What did I do to cause all this

A
grief? Now what'd I say to make you wan-na
B♭dim7
leave? Now wait a min - ute.
N.C.
Gave my heart and soul to you now
did-n't I? And did-n't I al-ways treat you good, now
Am
Am/G
did-n't I? I'm stand-ing in the shad-ows of love.
Fmaj7
E
I'm get - ting read - y for the heart-aches to come.
Try'n' my best to get read - y for the heart-aches to come.
E7
Repeat and Fade
Don't you see me

STOP! IN THE NAME OF LOVE

Words and Music by LAMONT DOZIER, BRIAN HOLLAND and EDWARD HOLLAND

Moving and steady
Am
G
F
Stop! In the name of love before you
G7
C
F
C
break my heart. (Instrumental)
F G C
Ba-by, ba-by, I'm a -
Em
Gm
3
ware of where you go each time you
A7
F
leave my door. I watch you walk
G7
F
down the street, know - ing your oth - er

G7
C
love you meet.
But this time before you
G
F
run to her
leav-ing me a-
lone to cry:
C
F
Have-n't I been
C
F
good to you?
Have-n't I been
C
Am
Am
sweet to you?
Stop! In the
G
F
G7
name of love
be-fore you break my heart,
Am
G
Stop! In the name of love

F
To Coda G7
be - fore you break my heart. Think it
C F C F G
o - ver, think it o - ver.
C
1
Em
I've known of your, your se - clud-ed nights,
Gm A7
I've e - ven seen her may - be once or twice.
F G7
But is her sweet ex - pres - sion
F G7
worth more than my love and af - fec - tion?
C G
This time be - fore you leave my arms

F
and rush off to her charms:
2
C
Em
I've tried so hard, hard to be pa - tient
Gm
A7
hop - ing you'd stop this in - fat - u - a - tion.
F
G7
But each time you are to - geth - er
F
G7
D.S. al Coda
I'm so a - fraid I'm los - ing you for - ev - er.
CODA
G7
Am
break my heart. Stop! In the
G
F
Repeat and Fade
name of love be - fore you

SUPERSTITION

Words and Music by
STEVIE WONDER

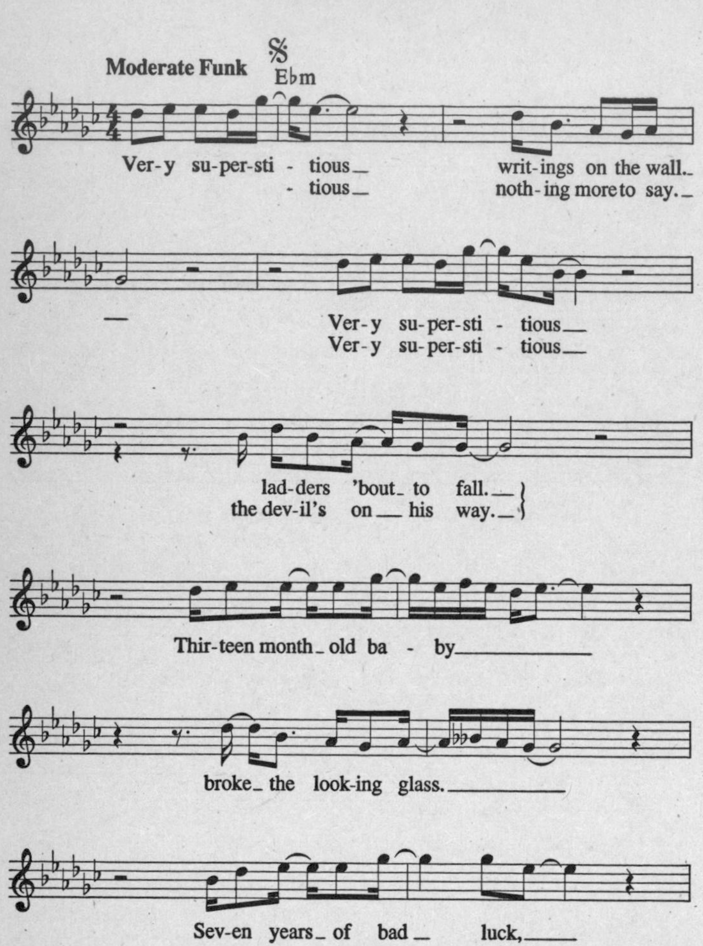
Moderate Funk
Ebm
Ver-y su-per-sti - tious_ writ-ings on the wall._
- tious_ noth-ing more to say._
Ver-y su-per-sti - tious_
Ver-y su-per-sti - tious_
lad-ders 'bout_ to fall._
the dev-il's on_ his way._
Thir-teen month_ old ba - by
broke_ the look-ing glass.
Sev-en years_ of bad_ luck,

the good things in your past.

B♭
C♭7
When you be - lieve in things that you don't

B♭
A7♭5
A♭
un- der - stand then you suf - fer.

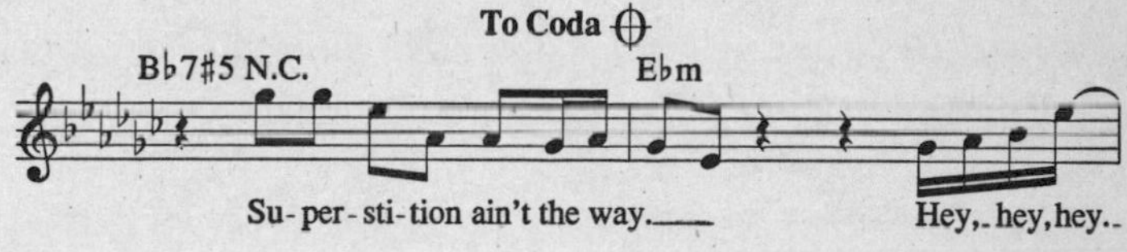
To Coda
B♭7#5 N.C.
E♭m
Su- per- sti- tion ain't the way.
Hey, hey, hey.

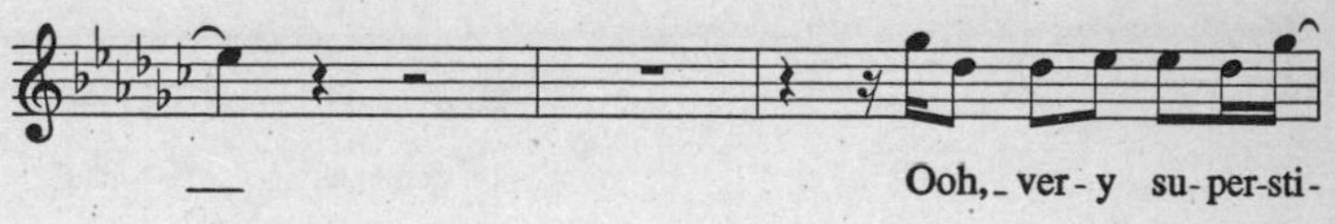
Ooh, ver - y su- per-sti-

- tious.
Wash your face and hands.

Rid me of the prob -

- lems,
do all
that you
3

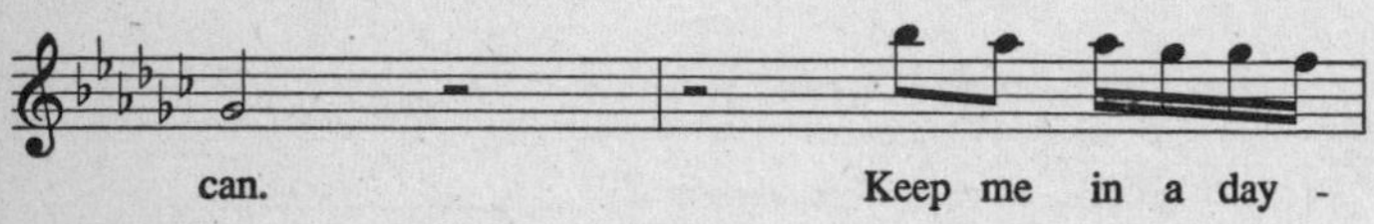
can.
Keep me in a day -

- dream,
3
keep me go-in' strong.

You don't wan - na save

me.
3
Sad is my song.

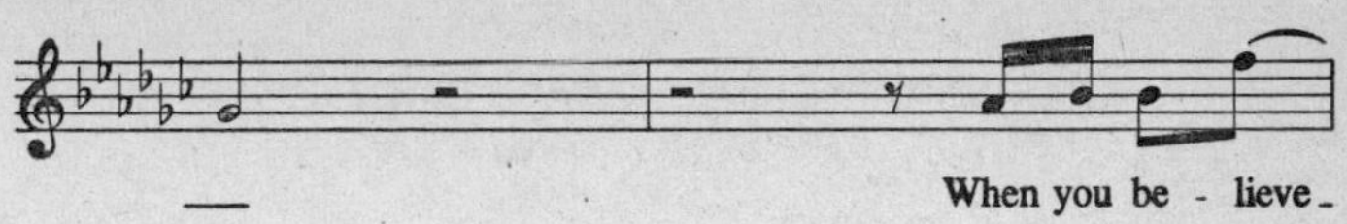
When you be - lieve

Bb
Cb7
Bb
A7b5
in things
you don't un - der - stand
then you suf -

Ab
fer.

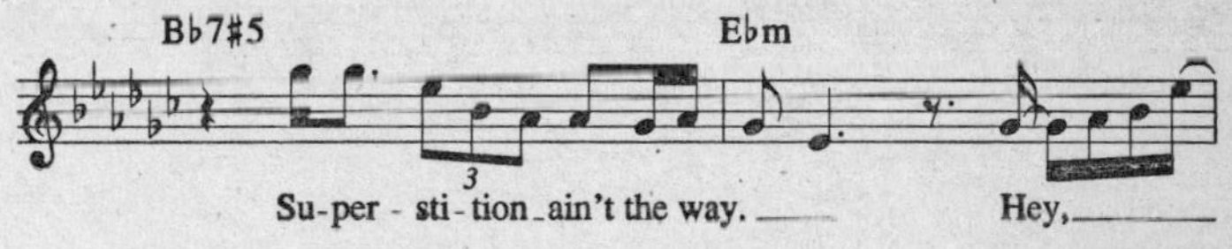
Bb7#5
Ebm
3
Su-per - sti-tion ain't the way.
Hey,

D.S. al Coda
yeah.
Ve-ry su-per-sti-

CODA
Ebm
Repeat and Fade

SWEET LOVE

Words and Music by GARY BIAS,
LOUIS A. JOHNSON and ANITA BAKER

Fmaj7
F/G
D/E
- in' out your name. I feel no shame; I'm in love.

Amaj7
Dm9
Sweet love, don't you ev -

F/G
D/E
- er go a - way. It - 'll al-ways be this way. Your

Amaj9
Dm9
heart has called me clos - er to you.

Fmaj9
Em7
F/G
D/E
I will be all that you need. Just trust

Amaj9
Dm9
in what we're feel - ing.

Fmaj9
F/G
D/E
Nev-er leave,_ 'cause ba-by I be-lieve_ in this love._

Amaj7
Dm9
Sweet_ love,__ hear me call__

Fmaj7
F/G
D/E
- in' out your name.__ I feel no shame; _I'm in love._

Amaj7
Dm9
Sweet_ love,__ don't you ev -

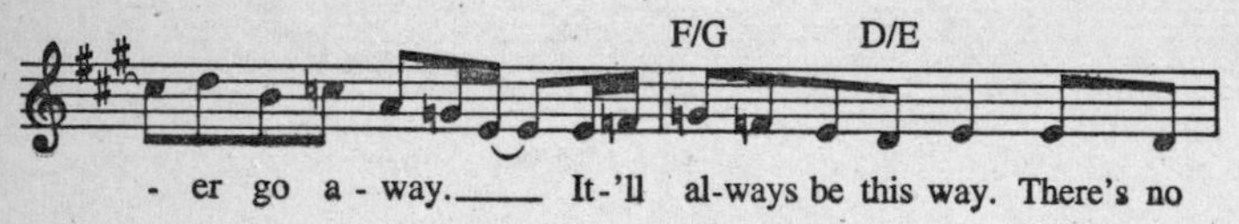
F/G
D/E
- er go a - way.___ It-'ll al-ways be this way. There's no

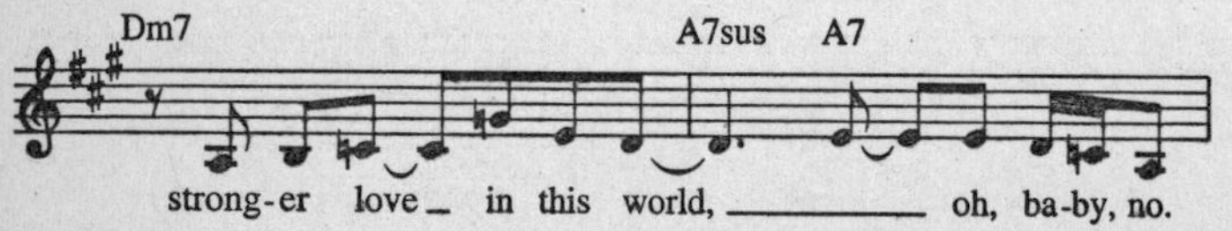
Dm7
A7sus
A7
strong-er love_ in this world,_____ oh, ba-by, no.

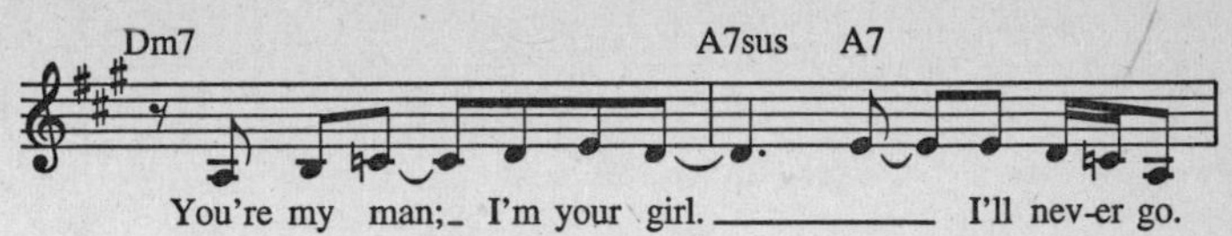
Dm7
A7sus
A7
You're my man; I'm your girl. I'll nev-er go.

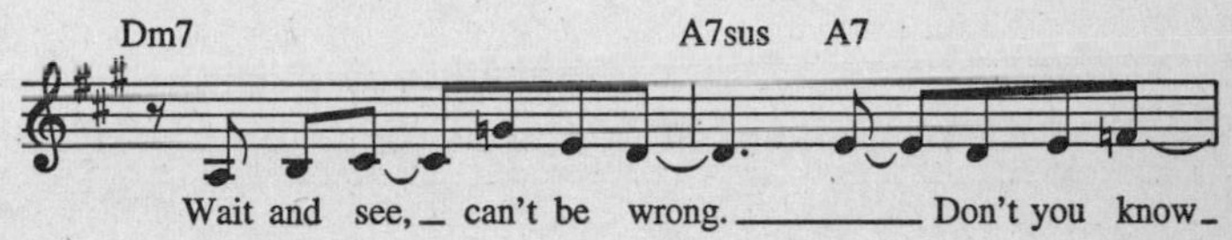
Dm7
A7sus
A7
Wait and see, can't be wrong. Don't you know

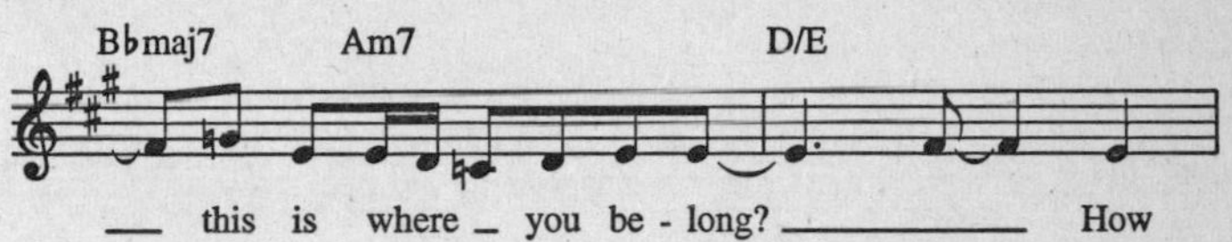
B♭maj7
Am7
D/E
this is where you be - long? How

Amaj9
Dm9
sweet this dream, how love - ly, ba - by.

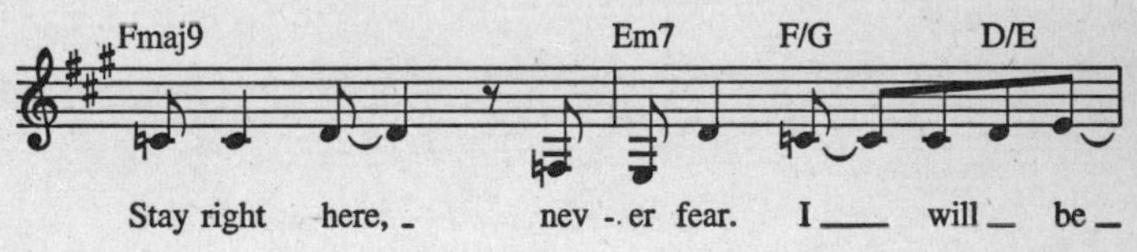
Fmaj9
Em7
F/G
D/E
Stay right here, nev - er fear. I will be

Amaj9
Dm9
all that you need.

Fmaj9
F/G
D/E
Nev-er leave, 'cause ba-by I be-lieve in this love.

Amaj7
Dm9
Sweet love, hear me call

Fmaj7
F/G
D/E
- in' out your name. I feel no shame; I'm in love.

Amaj7
Dm9
Sweet love, don't you ev -

F/G
D/E
- er go a - way. It-'ll al-ways be this way.

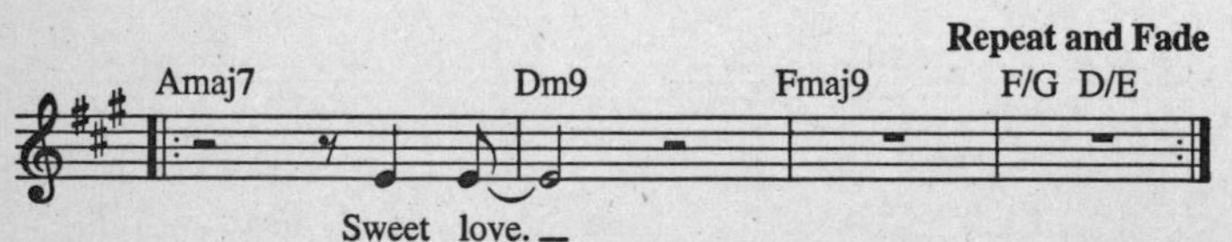
Repeat and Fade
Amaj7
Dm9
Fmaj9
F/G D/E
Sweet love.

TOO BUSY THINKING ABOUT MY BABY

Words and Music by JANIE BRADFORD, NORMAN WHITFIELD and BARRETT STRONG

Moderately
F Gm F Gm F
I ain't got time to think a - bout mon - ey
Gm F Gm F
or what it can buy, and
Gm F
I ain't got time to sit down and won - der
Gm F Gm Am
at what makes the bird-ies fly. I don't have time
B♭maj7 Am
to think a - bout what makes the flow - ers
B♭maj7 Am B♭maj7
grow, ain't nev - er give it a thought to

Gm7 F Gm7 F Gm F
where riv - ers flow.
Gm F
Ain't got time for noth-in' else.
Gm F Gm F
I ain't got time to dis - cuss the weath - er,
Gm F Gm7 F
or know what's go - ing on, and
Gm F Gm F
I ain't got time to do no stud - y - ing
Gm F Gm7 F Am
once I get out of class. And I'm just a
B♭maj7 Am
fel low with a one track mind,

B♭maj7
Am
3
and when it comes to think-in' a-bout
B♭maj7
Gm
3
an - y-thing but my ba - by, I just don't have time._
F Gm F Gm F Gm7 F
Ain't _ got time _ for noth-in'
Fine F Gm F Gm F
else. I ain't got time to read a news-pa - per
Gm F Gm F
or look at ___ T. V. ___ 'Cause
Gm F Gm F
I'm not con - cerned _ with what the fu - ture holds _
D.S. al Fine
Gm F Gm Am Asus
in store _ for me. I'm ___ just a

THREE TIMES A LADY

Words and Music by
LIONEL RICHIE

Slowly
Ab
Ab/Gb
Fm
Thanks for the times that you've giv - en me
C7#5/E
Ab
Ab/Gb
The mem-'ries are all in my mind
Fm
C7#5/E
Ab
And now that we've
Ab/Gb
Fm
C7#5/E
come to the end of our rain - bow
Ab
Ab/Gb
Fm
there's some-thing I must say out loud:
C7#5/E
Ab
You're once,

Eb/G
Gb
Db/F
twice, three times a la - dy
Bbm7
Ab
Eb
and I love you.
Eb/Db
Ab
Eb/G
Yes you're once, twice,
Gb
Db/F
Bbm7
three times a la - dy and I love
Ab
Eb
Eb/Db
Eb/C
you, I love
Eb/Bb
Ab
Eb/Ab
Ab
you.
Db/Eb
Ab
Eb/Ab
When we are to - geth - er the

Db6/Ab
Db/Eb
Ab
mo - ments I cher - ish with ev - 'ry beat
Eb/Ab
Db6/Ab
Db/Eb
of my heart, To
Ab
Eb/Ab
Db6/Ab
touch you, to hold you, to feel you, to
Db/Eb
Ab
Eb/Ab
need you, there's noth - ing to keep us a -
Db6/Ab
Db/Eb
Ab
part.
Eb/Ab
Db6/Ab
(Instrumental)
Eb/Ab
Db/Ab
Ab
Ooo

Eb/Ab
Db/Ab
— ooo ooo ooo
Ab
Eb/Ab
Db/Ab
ooo
ooo
Ab
You're once,
Eb/G
Gb
Db/F
twice, three times a la - dy
Bbm7
Ab
Eb
and I love you,
Eb/Db
Eb/C
Eb/Bb
I love
8va
Ab
you. (Instrumental)

TOUCH ME IN THE MORNING

Words and Music by RONALD MILLER and MICHAEL MASSER

Moderate ballad, expressively
D(add9)
Dmaj7
Touch me in the morn - ing,
morn - ing,
G(add9)
G
Em7/A
D(add9)
D
then just walk a - way.
then just close the door.
G(add9)
Em7/A
D(add9)
D
C/D
We don't have to - mor - row,
Leave me as you found me,
G
G(add9)
G
but we had yes - ter -
emp - ty like be -
C
Em7/A
day.
fore.
Dmaj7
D7
Hey! Was-n't it me who said that noth-in'
Hey! Was-n't it yes - ter - day we used to

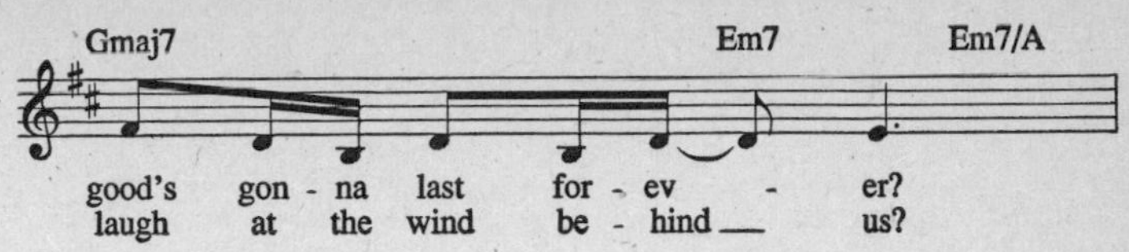
Gmaj7
Em7
Em7/A
good's gon - na last for - ev - er?
laugh at the wind be - hind __ us?

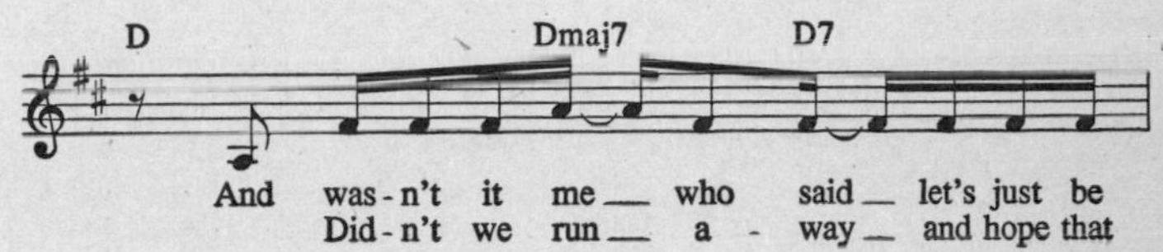
D
Dmaj7
D7
And was - n't it me __ who said __ let's just be
Did - n't we run __ a - way __ and hope that

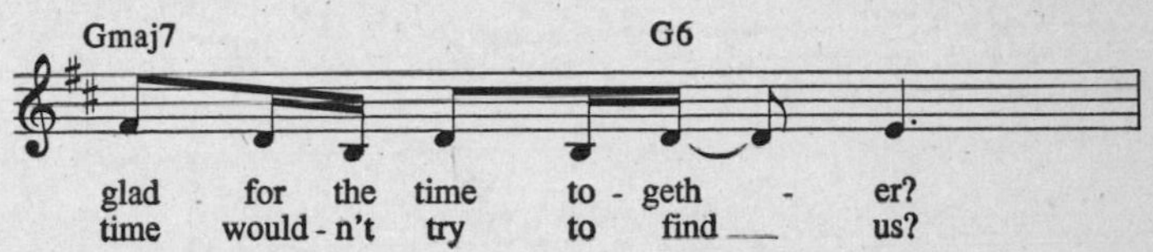
Gmaj7
G6
glad for the time to - geth - er?
time would - n't try to find __ us?

A/C#
Must - 've been hard __ to tell me,
Did - n't we take __ each oth - er,

C
that you've giv - en all __ you had __ to give.
to a place __ where no __ one's ev - er been?

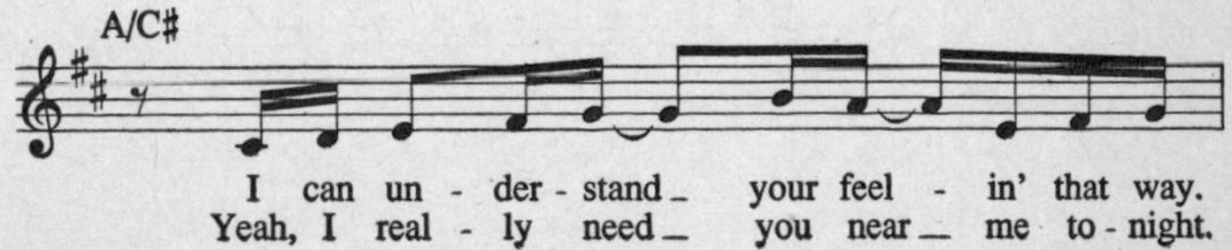
A/C#
I can un - der - stand __ your feel - in' that way.
Yeah, I real - ly need __ you near __ me to - night.

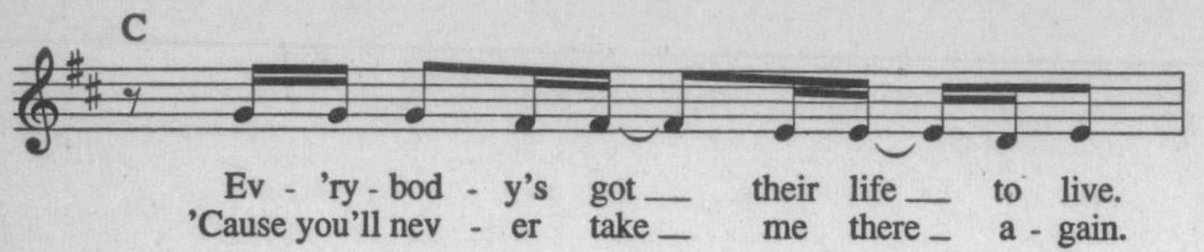
C
Ev - 'ry - bod - y's got their life to live.
'Cause you'll nev - er take me there a - gain.

Gmaj7
A/G
3
3
Well, I can say good - bye in the
Let me watch you go with the

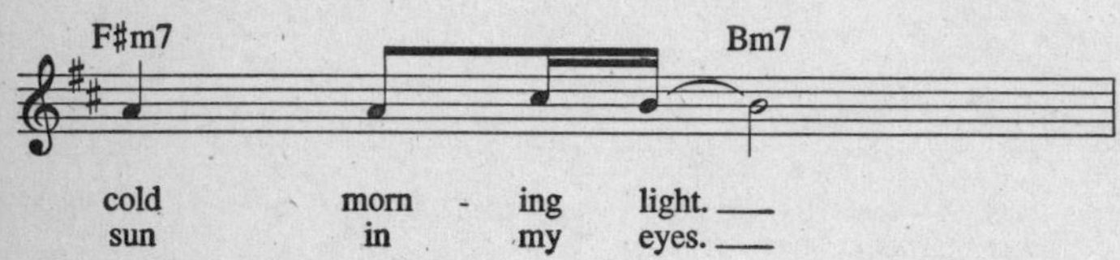
F#m7
Bm7
cold morn - ing light.
sun in my eyes.

Gmaj7
A/G
3
3
F#m7
Bm7
But I can't watch love die in the warmth of the night.
We've seen how love can grow, now we'll see how it dies.

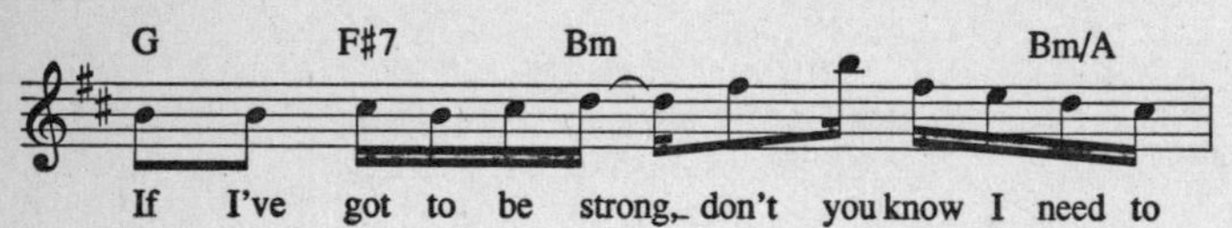
G
F#7
Bm
Bm/A
If I've got to be strong, don't you know I need to

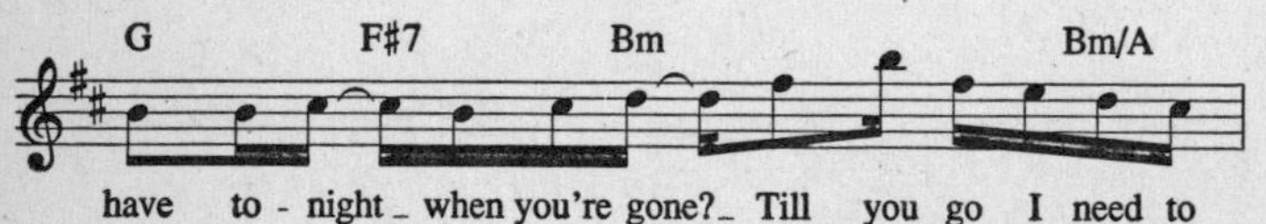
G
F#7
Bm
Bm/A
have to - night when you're gone? Till you go I need to

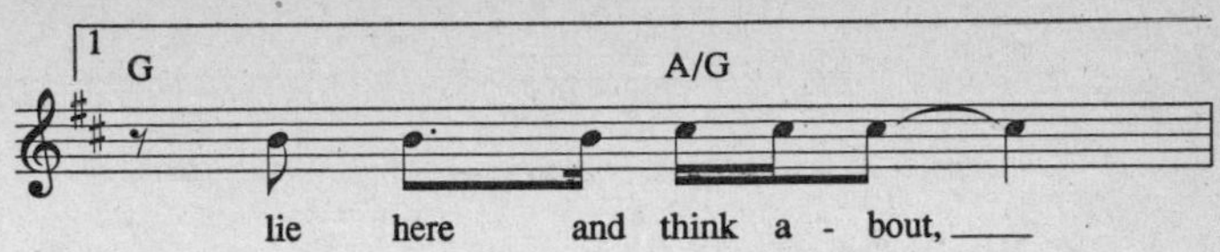
1
G
A/G
lie here and think a - bout,

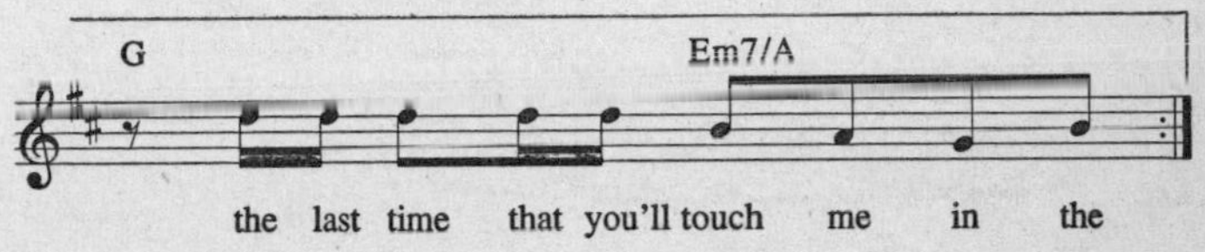
G
Em7/A
the last time that you'll touch me in the

2
G
A/G
hold you un - til the time,

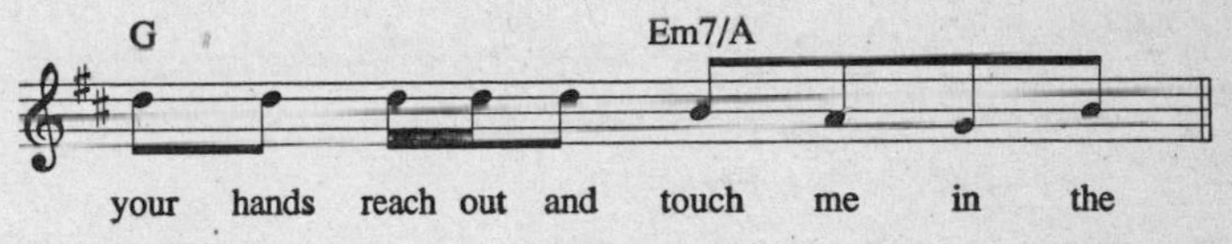
G
Em7/A
your hands reach out and touch me in the

D(add9)
D
Dmaj7
D7
Duet:
Morn - ing.
Morn-ings were blue and gold and we could
Gmaj7
Em7
Em7/A
Then just walk a -
feel one an - oth - er liv - ing.

D(add9)
D
Dmaj7
D7
way.
We walked_with a dream_ to hold_ and we could
Gmaj7
Em7
Em7/A
take what the world was giv - ing. ___
We don't have to -
D(add9)
D
Dmaj7
D7
mor - row.
There's no to - mor - row here,_ there's on - ly
Gmaj7
G6
love and the time to chase_ it. ___
But we had yes - ter -
C
day.
Yes - ter - day's gone_ my love,_ there's on - ly
Em7/A
Repeat and Fade
now and it's time to face_ it. ___
Touch me in the

THE TRACKS OF MY TEARS

Words and Music by WILLIAM "SMOKEY" ROBINSON, WARREN MOORE and MARVIN TARPLIN

Moderately
G C D
Do, do, do, doot. Do, do, do, doot. Do, do, do,
G C Bm Am G
doot. Do, do, do, do, do, do.
C D
People say I'm the life of the party 'cause
Since you left me, if you see me with another girl,
G C G Am7 G
I tell a joke or two. Although I
seemin' like I'm havin' fun. Although she
C D
might be laughin' loud and hearty,
may be cute, she's just a substitute because
G C G Am7 G
deep inside I'm blue.
you're the permanent one.
So take a

C
D
G
C
3
good look at my face. You'll see my smile looks out of
G
C
3
place.
If you look clos - er
Look a lit - tle bit clos - er,
it's eas - y to
D
G
C
trace the tracks of my tears.
G Am7 G
C
G
I need you, need
1
C G
2
N.C.
you.
you.
C G
C
G
C G
Hey, hey, yeah. (Out - side.) I'm mas-quer-
C
G
C
G
ad - ing. (In - side,) my hope is

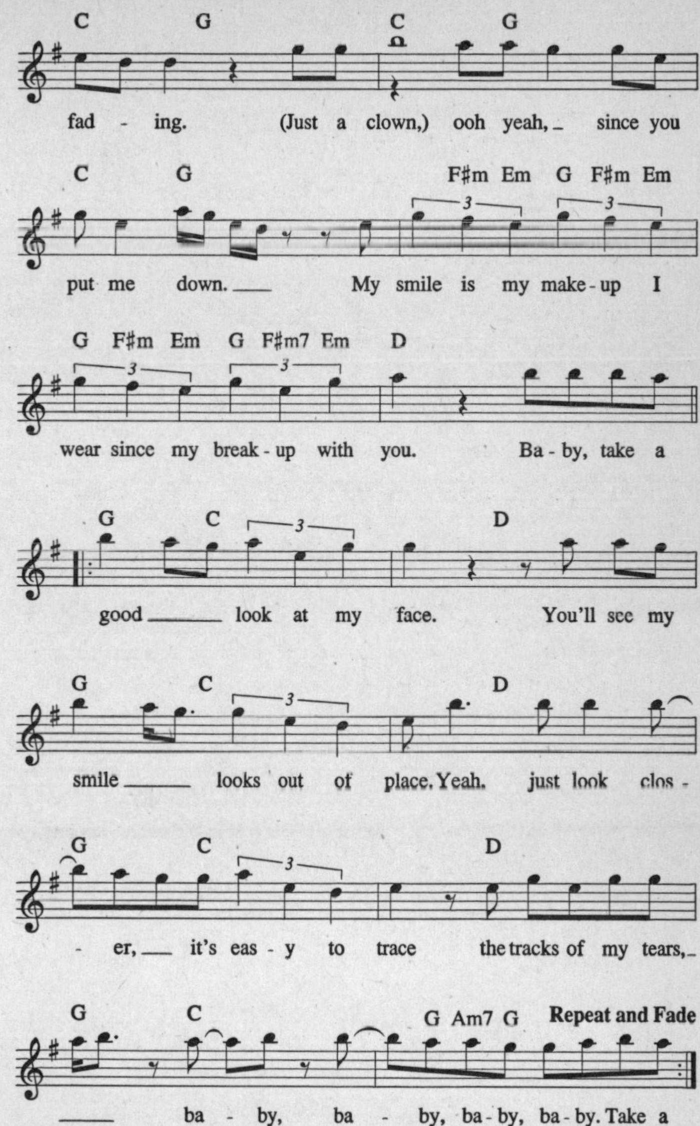
C G C G
fad - ing. (Just a clown,) ooh yeah, since you
C G F♯m Em G F♯m Em
put me down. My smile is my make - up I
G F♯m Em G F♯m7 Em D
wear since my break - up with you. Ba - by, take a
G C D
good look at my face. You'll see my
G C D
smile looks out of place. Yeah. just look clos -
G C D
- er, it's eas - y to trace the tracks of my tears,
G C G Am7 G
Repeat and Fade
ba - by, ba - by, ba - by, ba - by. Take a

WAR

Words and Music by NORMAN WHITFIELD
and BARRETT STRONG

Slow Rock (with double time feel)

Fm Ab Gm7/C
1. War, uh! What is it
2., 3. See additional lyrics

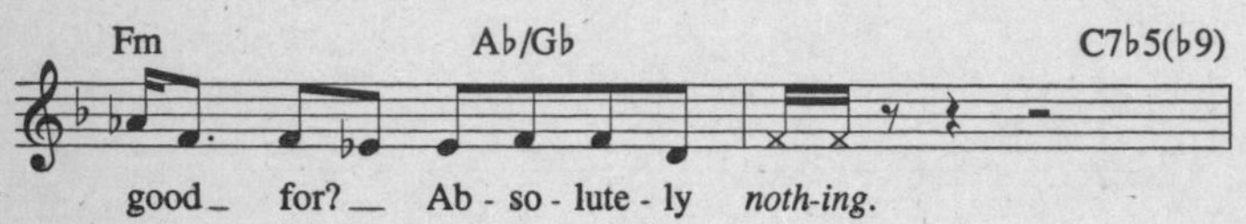
Fm Ab/Gb C7b5(b9)
good_ for?_ Ab-so-lute-ly noth-ing.

Fm Ab Gm7/C
War, uh! What is it

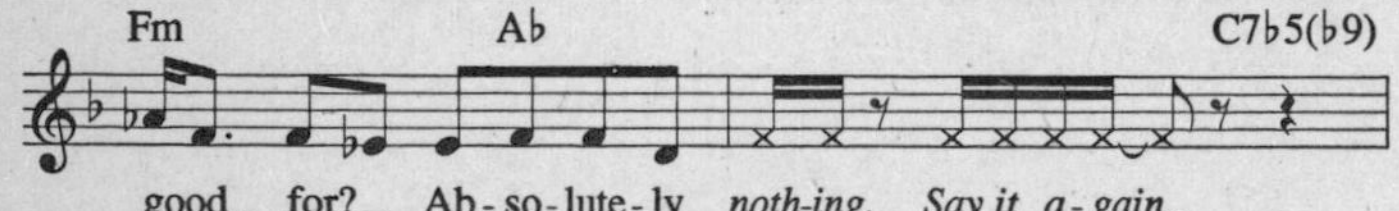
Fm Ab C7b5(b9)

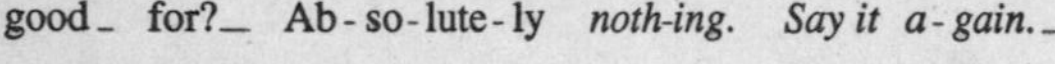
good_ for?_ Ab-so-lute-ly noth-ing. Say it a-gain._

Fm Ab Gm7/C Fm Ab
War, uh! What is it good_ for? Ab-so-lute-ly

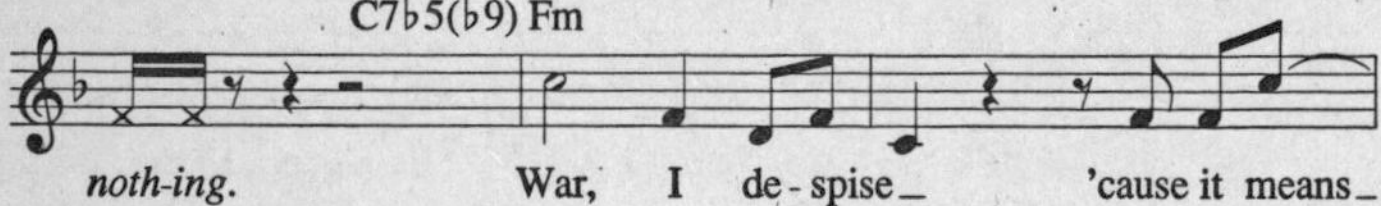
C7b5(b9) Fm
noth-ing. War, I de-spise_ 'cause it means_

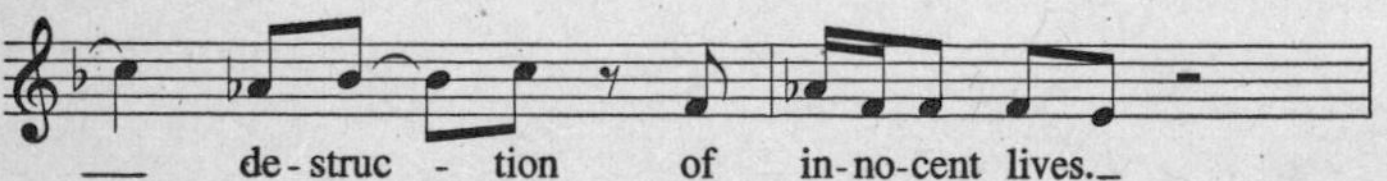
_ de-struc - tion of in-no-cent lives._

War means tears in thou - sands of moth-ers' eyes when their

Fade on last repeat

sons go out to fight and lose their lives. I said

Additional Lyrics

2. War, uh! What is it good for? Absolutely nothing; say it again;
   War, uh! What is it good for? Absolutely nothing.
   War, it's nothing but a heartbreaker; War, friend only to the undertaker.
   War is an enemy to all mankind. The thought of War blows my mind.
   War has caused unrest within the younger generation;
   Induction then destruction, who wants to die? Ah
   War, uh um; What is it good for? You tell me nothing, um!
   War, uh! What is it good for? Absolutely nothing.
   Good God, war, it's nothing but a heartbreaker;
   War, friend only to the undertaker.

3. Wars have shattered many a young man's dreams;
   Made him disabled, bitter and mean.
   Life is much too short and precious to spend fighting wars each day.
   War can't give life, it can only take it away. Ah
   War, uh um! What is it good for? Absolutely nothing, um.
   War, good God almighty, listen, what is it good for? Absolutely nothing, yeah.
   War, it's nothing but a heartbreaker; War, friend only to the undertaker.
   Peace, love and understanding, tell me is there no place for them today?
   They say we must fight to keep our freedom,
   but Lord knows it's gotta be a better way.
   I say War, uh um, yeah, yeah. What is it good for?
   Absolutely nothing; say it again;
   War, yea, yea, yea, yea, what is it good for? Absolutely nothing; say it again;
   War, nothing but a heartbreaker; What is it good for?
   Friend only to the undertaker....
   (Fade)

THE WAY YOU DO THE THINGS YOU DO

Words and Music by WILLIAM "SMOKEY" ROBINSON
and ROBERT ROGERS

G C/G G C/G G C/G G C/G
The way you smell so sweet,
And Ba - by you're so smart,
G C/G G C/G G C/G G C/G
you know you could - 've been some per - fume.
you know you could - 've been a school book.
D
Well, you could - 've been an - y-thing that you
C D
want - ed to and I can tell
C G C/G G C/G
the way you do the things you do. Ah, Ba -
1
G C/G G C/G G
- by. As pret - ty as you
2
G C/G G C/G G
- by. Yes!

WHAT'S GOING ON

Words and Music by MARVIN GAYE,
AL CLEVELAND and RENALDO BENSON

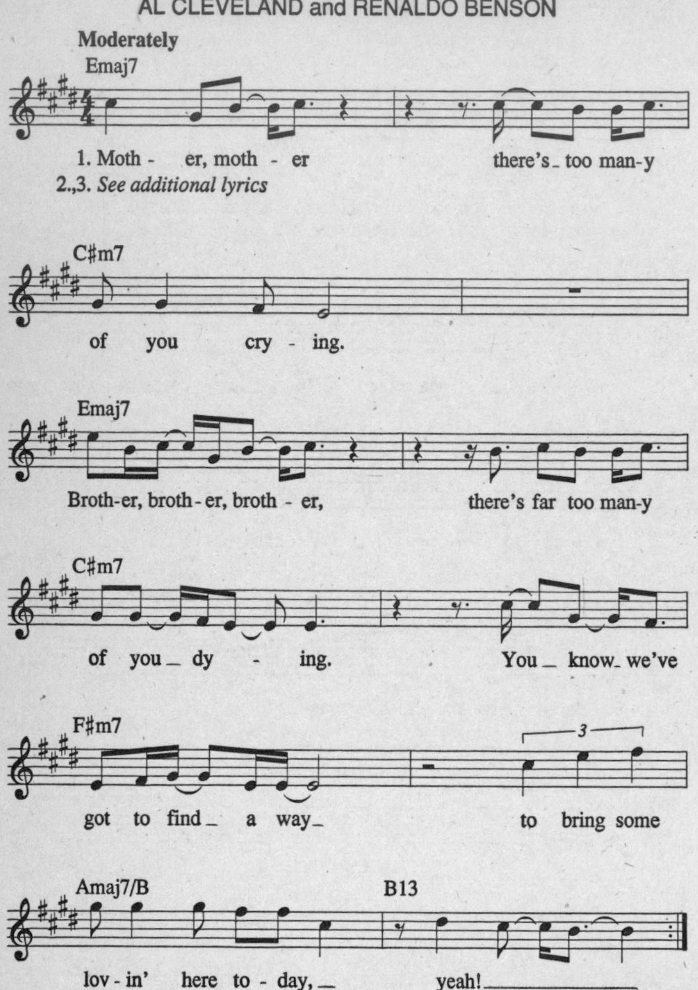
Moderately
Emaj7
1. Moth - er, moth - er there's too man-y
2.,3. See additional lyrics
C#m7
of you cry - ing.
Emaj7
Broth-er, broth-er, broth - er, there's far too man-y
C#m7
of you dy - ing. You know we've
F#m7
got to find a way to bring some
3
Amaj7/B
B13
lov - in' here to - day, yeah!

Chorus
F♯m7
Amaj7/B
Pick-et lines_ and pick-et signs,_ don't
F♯m7
Amaj7/B
pun-ish me with_ bru - tal - i - ty;
F♯m7
Amaj7/B
B13
talk to me so you can see; oh, what's
Emaj7
C♯m7
go-ing on. What's go ing on ____ yeah,_ what's
Emaj7
C♯m7
go-ing on, ____ oh, what's go-ing on. ____ Ah ___
Am9
ah, ah, ah. ___
I _____ yi, yi, yi, ___ yi, yi, ___ yi, yi, ___

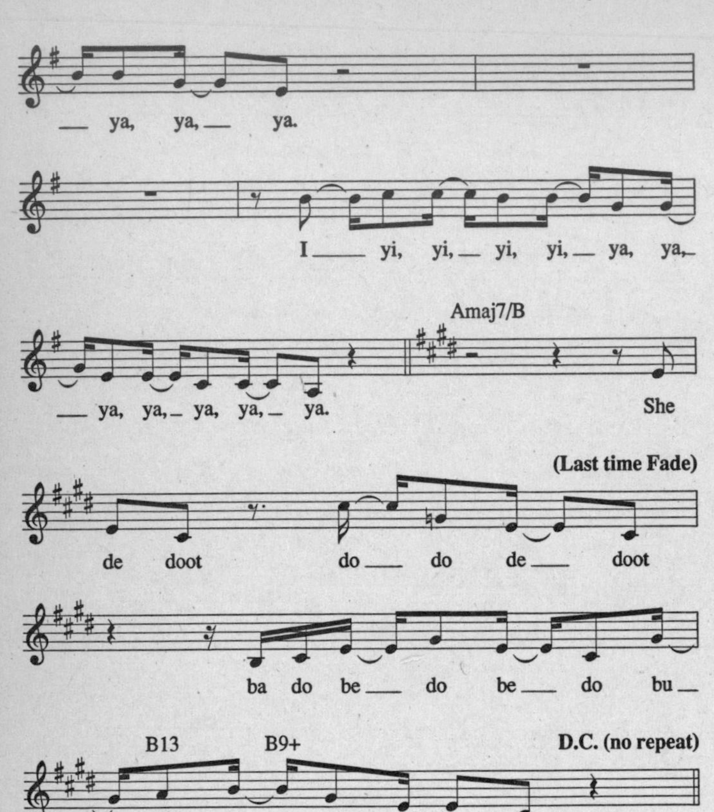

Additional Lyrics

2. Father, father we don't need to escalate
You see, war is not the answer for only love can conquer hate
You know we've got to find a way to bring some lovin' here today.
Chorus

3. Father, father everybody thinks we're wrong
Oh but, who are they to judge us simply because our hair is long?
Oh you know we've got to find a way to bring some understanding here today.
Chorus

WHERE DID OUR LOVE GO

Words and Music by BRIAN HOLLAND,
LAMONT DOZIER and EDWARD HOLLAND

G/F
C
You came in - to my heart (ba - by ba - by)
ren-der (ba - by ba - by)
3
G
so tell me with a burn-ing love
so help me sweet you now want to
Dm
1
(ba - by ba - by) that stings like a
leave. (ba - by ba - by)
G
bee. (ba - by ba - by) Now that I sur -
2
Dm7
G
Ooh, you wan - na leave me (ba - by ba - by)
G/F
C
ooh. (ba - by ba - by) Ba - by ba - by
(Instrumental)
G
F♯
where did our love go? Ooh, don't you

Dm7
want me; Don't you want me no
(ba - by ba - by)
G
1
G/F
more ba - by, ba - by? Ooh, ba - by.
2
G/F
D.C. al Coda
CODA
G/F
Be - fore you won my
C
heart (ba - by ba - by) you were a per - fect
G
guy; but now that you
Dm7
got me you wan - na leave me be -
(ba - by ba - by)
G
D.C. and Fade
hind ba - by, ba - by, ooh ba - by.
(ba - by ba - by)

YESTER-ME, YESTER-YOU, YESTERDAY

Words by RON MILLER
Music by BRYAN WELLS

Moderately
Dm7
G7
1. What hap - pened to
2. (See additional lyrics)
(D.S.) seems
C
the world we knew,
those yes - ter - dreams
Dm7
G7
when we would dream and scheme and
were just a cruel and fool - ish
C
E7
Am
while the time a - way,
game we used to play,
Yes - ter -
D7
G7
me, Yes - ter - you, Yes - ter -

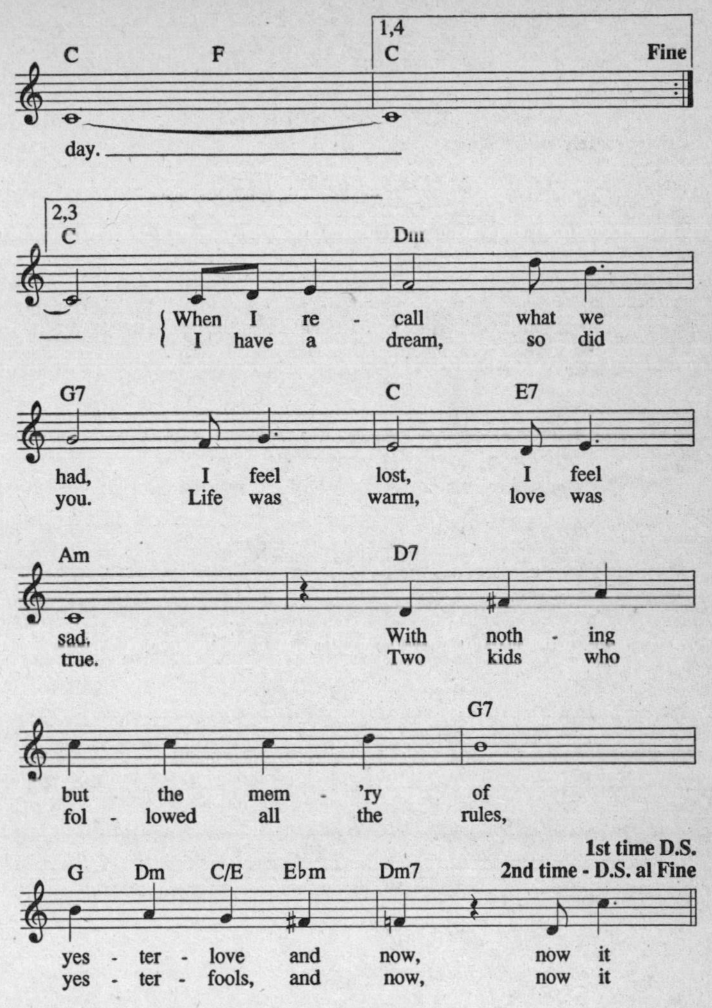
1,4
C F C Fine
day.
2,3
C Dm
When I re - call what we
I have a dream, so did
G7 C E7
had, I feel lost, I feel
you. Life was warm, love was
Am D7
sad, With noth - ing
true. Two kids who
G7
but the mem - 'ry of
fol - lowed all the rules,
1st time D.S.
G Dm C/E E♭m Dm7 2nd time - D.S. al Fine
yes - ter - love and now, now it
yes - ter - fools, and now, now it

Additional Lyrics

2. Where did it go, that yester-glow
When we could feel the wheel of life turn our way.
Yester-me, yester-you, yesterday.

YOU ARE THE SUNSHINE OF MY LIFE

Words and Music by
STEVIE WONDER

C Dm7 Dm7/G C
I feel like this
You must have known
F6 F/G Cmaj7 Fmaj9 F/G
in the be gin ning,
that I was lone - ly,
Cmaj7 F6 F/G
'though I've loved you for a mil - lion years.
be - cause you came to my res - cue.
Bm7♭5 E7 A
And if I thought
And I know that
D E Am9
our love was end - ing,
this must be heav - en;
D7
I'd find my - self, drown -
how could so much love be
- ing in my own
in - side of
G7
3rd time
Repeat and Fade
tears. Whoa, whoa.
you? Whoa.

YOU CAN'T HURRY LOVE

Words and Music by EDWARD HOLLAND, LAMONT DOZIER and BRIAN HOLLAND

Moderately bright
B♭
I need love, love ___ to
E♭ B♭ Dm Gm7
ease my mind; I need to find, find _ some-one to
E♭6 F7
call mine; but Ma - ma said ___ you
B♭ E♭ B♭
can't hur - ry love, _ no you just have to wait, _ she said
can't hur - ry love, _ no you just have to wait, _ she said
Dm Gm7 E♭ F7
love don't come ea - sy, ___ it's a game of give and take. _ You
love don't come ea - sy, ___ it's a game of give and take. _ How
B♭ E♭ B♭
can't hur - ry love, _ no, you just have to wait, _ you got - ta
long must I wait _ how much more can I take, _ be - fore

Dm
Gm
trust, give it time, no
lone - li - ness will
E♭
F7
Dm
mat - ter how long it takes; but how man - y heart-aches must I
'cause my heart, heart to break? No, I can't bear to live my
Gm
stand be - fore I find a love to let me
life a - lone. I grow im - pa - tient for a love to
live a - gain. Right now the
call my own; but when I
E♭
on - ly thing that keeps me
feel that I, I
F7
hang - ing on, when I feel my strength, yeah, it's
can't go on, these pre - cious words keep me
E♭/F
al - most gone, I re - mem - ber Ma - ma said,
hang - ing on; I re - mem - ber Ma - ma said,

B♭
can't hur - ry love, no, you
can't hur - ry love, no, you
E♭ B♭ Dm Gm
just have to wait, she said love don't come ea - sy
just have to wait, she said trust, give it time, no
1
E♭ F7
it's a game of give and take. You
2
E♭ F7 B♭
mat - ter how long it takes. No
E♭ B♭
love, love don't come ea - sy, but I
Dm Gm7 E♭ F7
keep on wait - ing, an - ti - ci - pat - ing for that
B♭ E♭ B♭
soft voice to talk to me at night, for some

Dm
Gm7
ten - der arms ___ to
E♭
F7
B♭
hold _ me tight. _ I keep wait-ing; I keep on
E♭
B♭
Dm
Gm
wait - ing, _ but it ain't ea - sy, _ it ain't
E♭
F7
ea - sy when Ma - ma said you
B♭
E♭
B♭
can't hur - ry love, _ no, you just have to wait; she said
See additional lyrics
Repeat and Fade
Dm
Gm
E♭
F7
trust, ___ give it time no mat - ter how long it takes. You

Additional Lyrics

You can't hurry love
You just have to wait,
She said love don't come easy
It's a game of give and take.

YOU KEEP ME HANGIN' ON

Words and Music by EDWARD HOLLAND, LAMONT DOZIER and BRIAN HOLLAND

1
B♭/C
Why do you keep a com - in' a - round
F
C
play - ing with my heart?
B♭/C
Why don't cha get out of my life
F
C
Em/B
and let me make a new start?
G
Let me get o - ver you the
E
way you've got - ten o - ver me.
2
B♭/C
You say al - though we broke up you

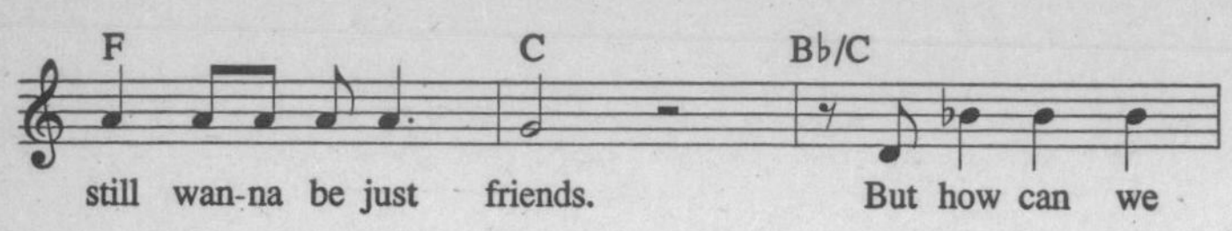
F
C
B♭/C
still wan-na be just friends. But how can we

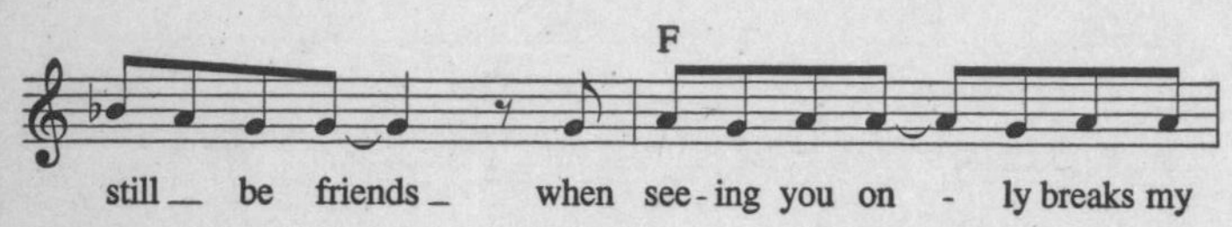
F
still __ be friends __ when see-ing you on - ly breaks my

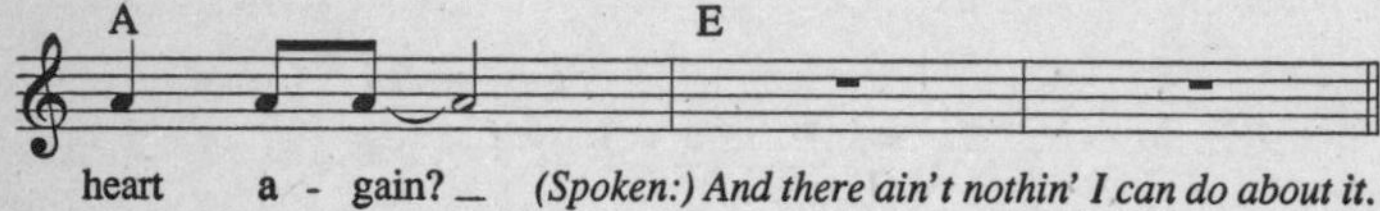
A
E
heart a - gain? __ (Spoken:) And there ain't nothin' I can do about it.

A
Em/G
Set me free why don't cha ba - by,

Em/D
Fmaj7
Esus
get out my life __ why don't __ cha ba - by. __

B♭/C
You claim __ you still __ care __ for me __ but your

F
C
heart and soul needs to be free. __________

B♭/C
Now that you've got your free - dom you
F
C
Em/B
wan - na still hold on to me.
G
You don't want me for your - self so
E
Am
let me find some-bod - y else.
A
Em/G
Why don't cha be a man a bout it
Em/D
Fmaj7
Esus
and set me free. Now
A
Em/G
you don't care a thing a - bout me,

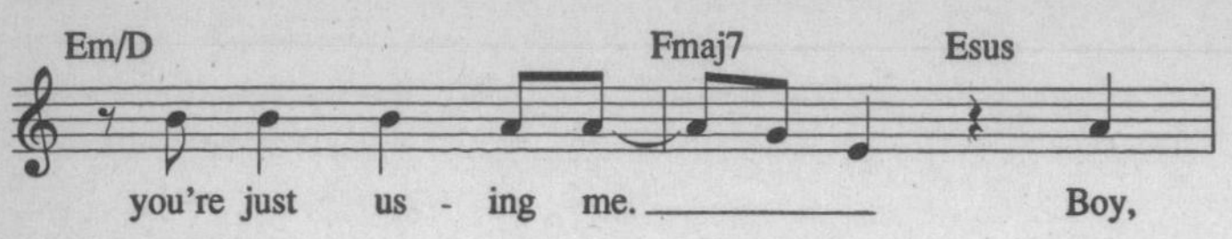
Em/D
Fmaj7
Esus
you're just us - ing me.
Boy,

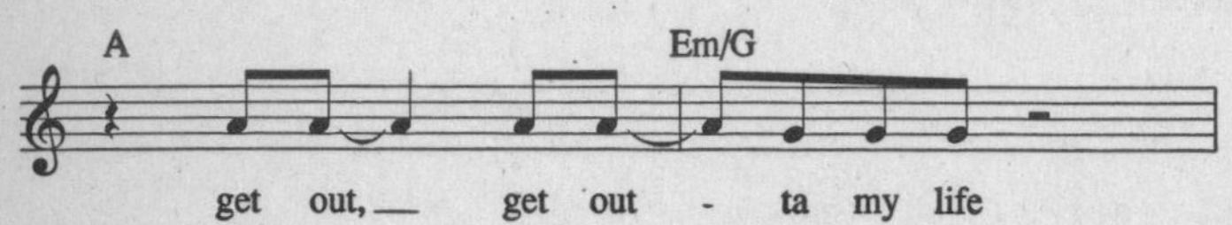
A
Em/G
get out, get out - ta my life

Em/D
Fmaj7
Esus
and let me sleep at night,

A
Em/G
'cause you don't real - ly love me, you just keep

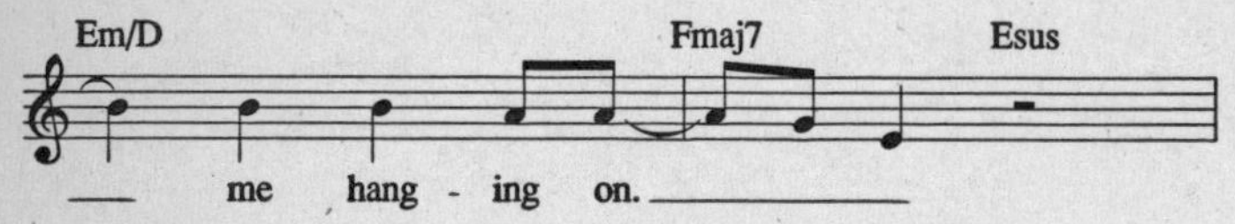
Em/D
Fmaj7
Esus
me hang - ing on.

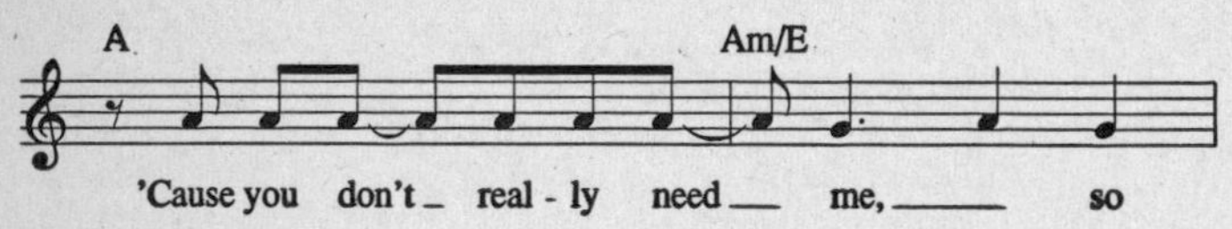
A
Am/E
'Cause you don't real - ly need me, so

Em/G
F
Am
let me be, set me free.

YOU'VE REALLY GOT A HOLD ON ME

Words and Music by
WILLIAM "SMOKEY" ROBINSON

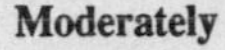
Moderately

C
3
3
I don't like you ___ but I love you,
I don't want you ___ but I need you,

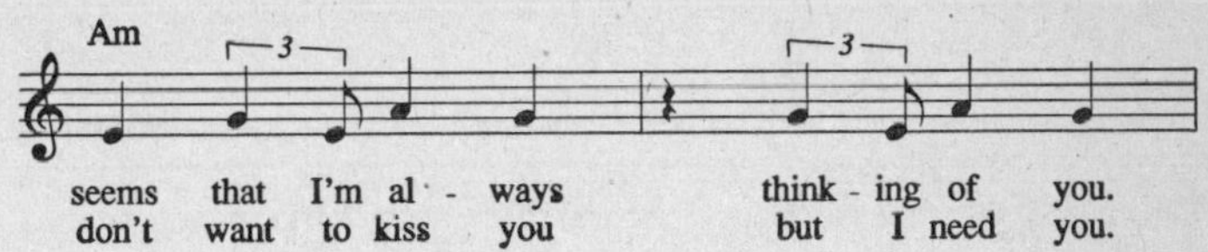
Am
3
3
seems that I'm al - ways think - ing of you.
don't want to kiss you but I need you.

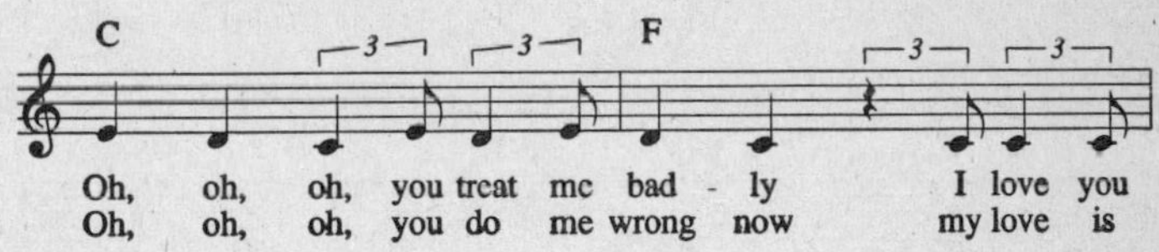
C
F
3
3
3
3
Oh, oh, oh, you treat me bad - ly I love you
Oh, oh, oh, you do me wrong now my love is

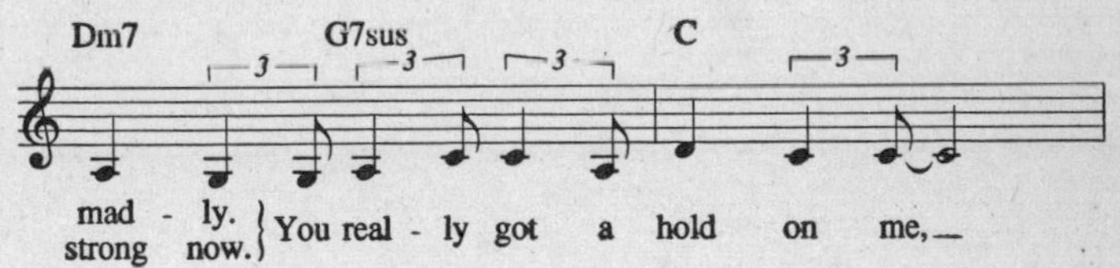
Dm7
G7sus
C
3
3
3
3
mad - ly.
strong now.
You real - ly got a hold on me, ___

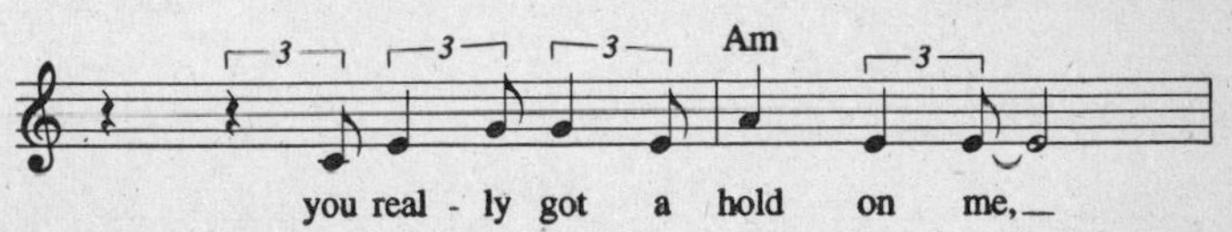
Am
3
3
3
3
you real - ly got a hold on me, ___

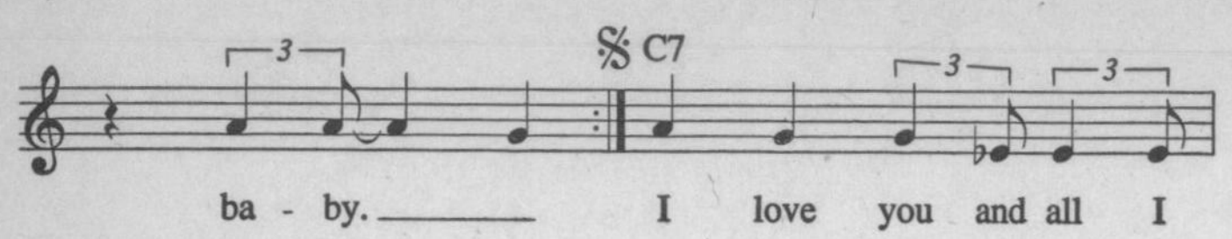
3
C7
3
3
ba - by.
I love you and all I

F7
3
3
C
want you to do is just hold me, hold me,

G7
3
To Coda
3
3
hold me, hold me.
(Instrumental)
You

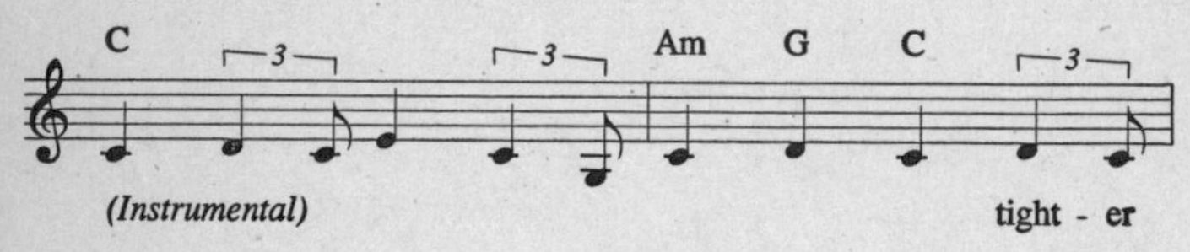
C
3
3
Am G C
3
(Instrumental)
tight - er

3
3
Am G7 Am
3
(Instrumental)
tight - er

C
3
3
3
3
I want to leave you don't want to stay here,

Am
3
3
3
don't want to spend ___ a-noth - er day here.

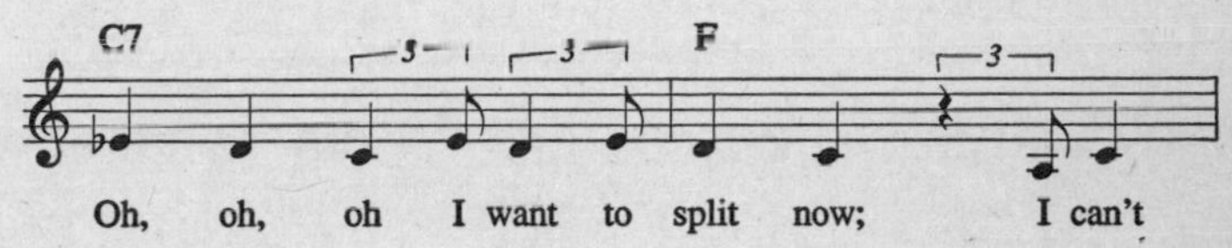
C7
3
3
F
3
Oh, oh, oh I want to split now; I can't

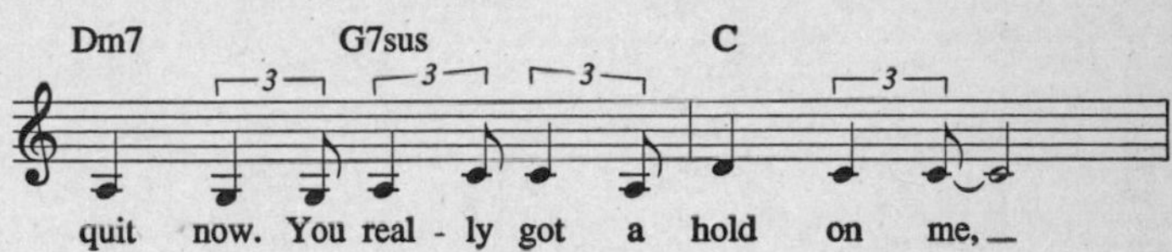
Dm7
G7sus
C
3
3
3
3
quit now. You real - ly got a hold on me, ___

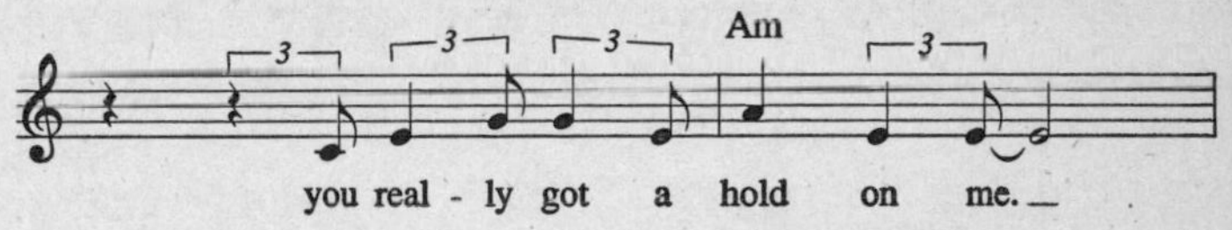
Am
3
3
3
3
you real - ly got a hold on me. ___

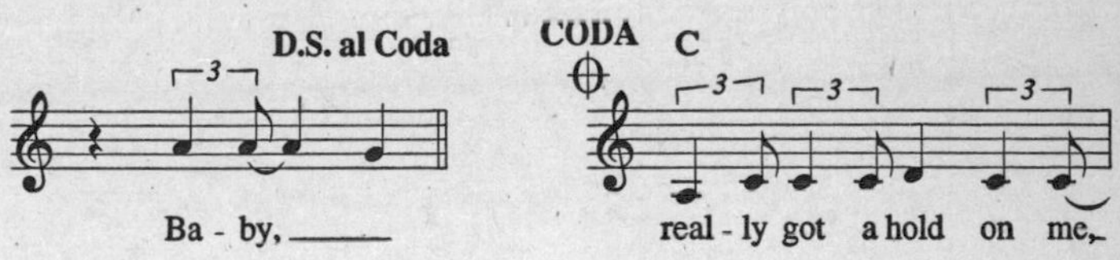
D.S. al Coda
CODA
C
3
3
3
3
Ba - by, ___
real - ly got a hold on me, ___

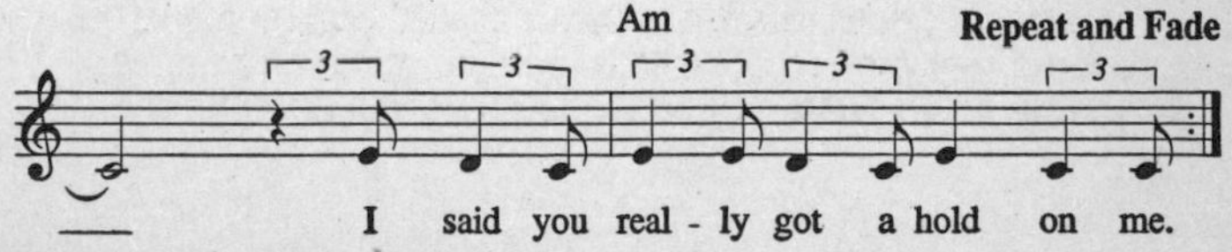
Am
Repeat and Fade
3
3
3
3
3
___ I said you real - ly got a hold on me.

GUITAR CHORD FRAMES

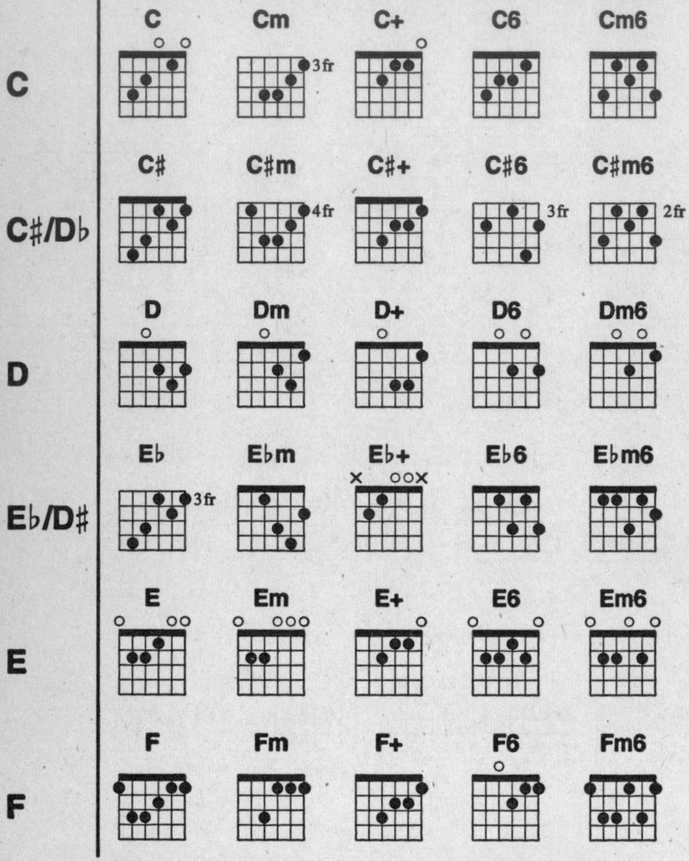

C	C	Cm (3fr)	C+	C6	Cm6
C♯/D♭	C♯	C♯m (4fr)	C♯+	C♯6 (3fr)	C♯m6 (2fr)
D	D	Dm	D+	D6	Dm6
E♭/D♯	E♭ (3fr)	E♭m	E♭+	E♭6	E♭m6
E	E	Em	E+	E6	Em6
F	F	Fm	F+	F6	Fm6

This guitar chord reference includes 120 commonly used chords. For a more complete guide to guitar chords, see "THE PAPERBACK CHORD BOOK" (HL00702009).

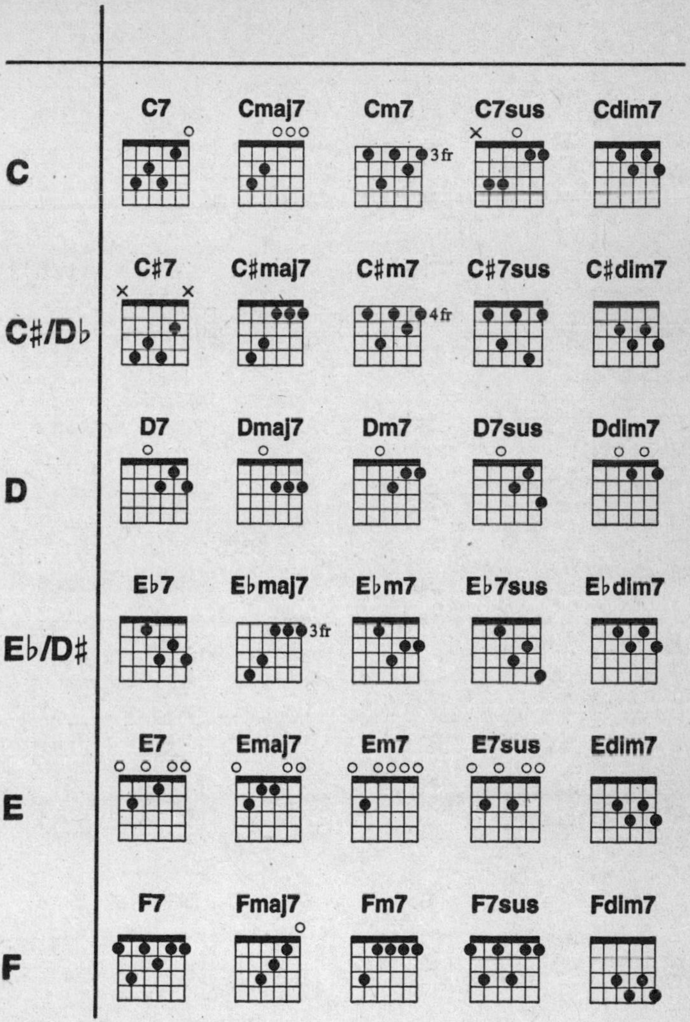

C	C7	Cmaj7	Cm7 (3fr)	C7sus	Cdim7
C♯/D♭	C♯7	C♯maj7	C♯m7 (4fr)	C♯7sus	C♯dim7
D	D7	Dmaj7	Dm7	D7sus	Ddim7
E♭/D♯	E♭7	E♭maj7 (3fr)	E♭m7	E♭7sus	E♭dim7
E	E7	Emaj7	Em7	E7sus	Edim7
F	F7	Fmaj7	Fm7	F7sus	Fdim7

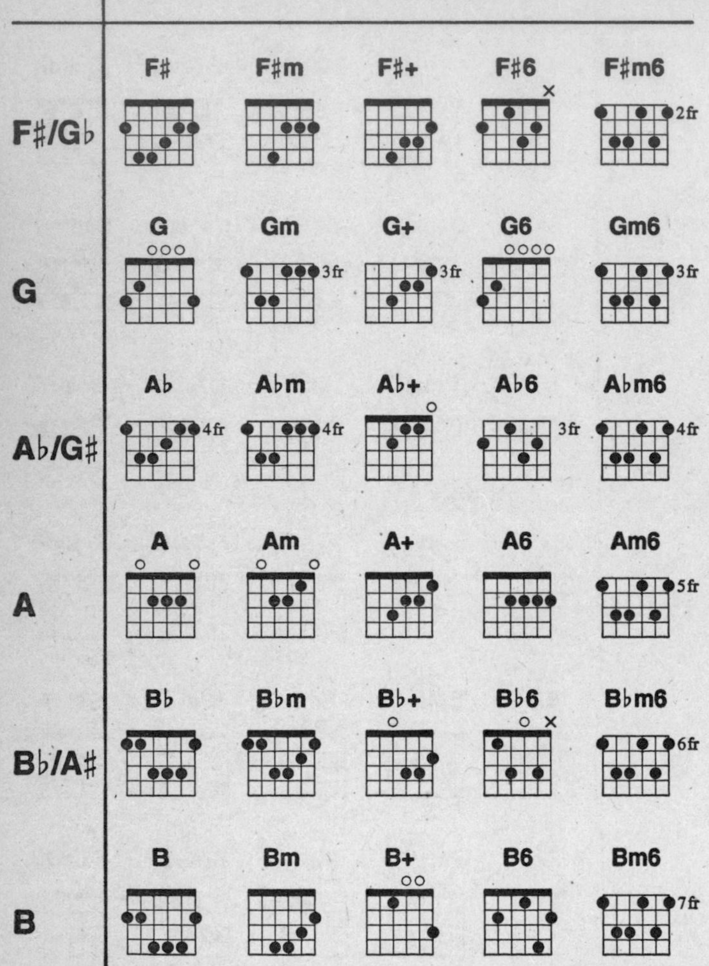
F♯/G♭
F♯
F♯m
F♯+
F♯6
F♯m6
2fr
G
G
Gm
3fr
G+
3fr
G6
Gm6
3fr
A♭/G♯
A♭
4fr
A♭m
4fr
A♭+
A♭6
3fr
A♭m6
4fr
A
A
Am
A+
A6
Am6
5fr
B♭/A♯
B♭
B♭m
B♭+
B♭6
B♭m6
6fr
B
B
Bm
B+
B6
Bm6
7fr

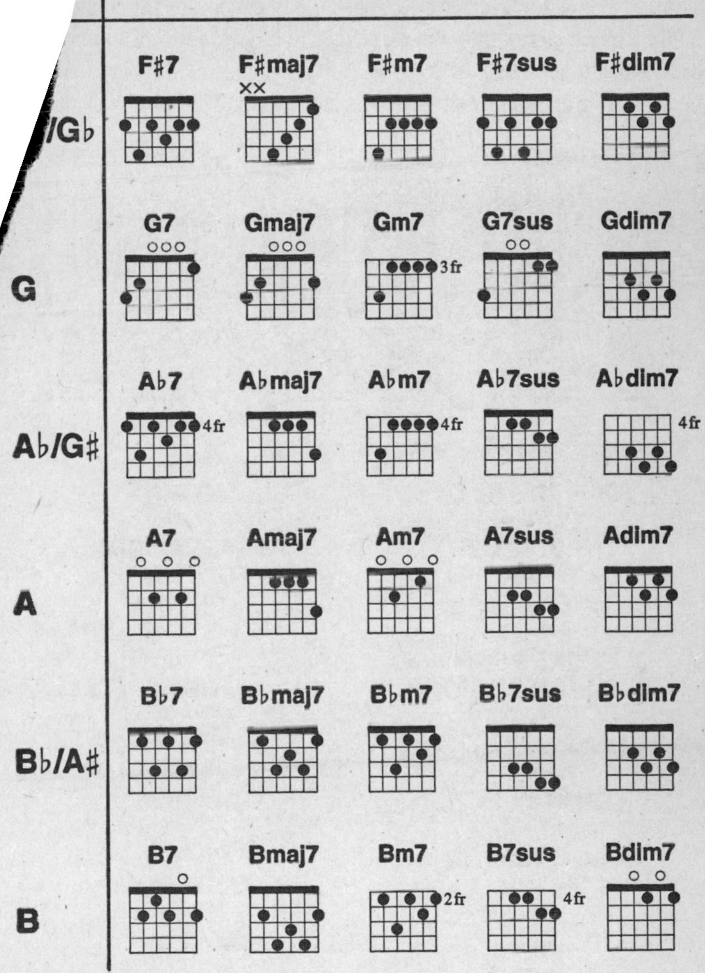
F♯/G♭
F♯7
F♯maj7
F♯m7
F♯7sus
F♯dim7
G
G7
Gmaj7
Gm7
3 fr
G7sus
Gdim7
A♭/G♯
A♭7
4 fr
A♭maj7
A♭m7
4 fr
A♭7sus
A♭dim7
4 fr
A
A7
Amaj7
Am7
A7sus
Adim7
B♭/A♯
B♭7
B♭maj7
B♭m7
B♭7sus
B♭dim7
B
B7
Bmaj7
Bm7
2 fr
B7sus
4 fr
Bdim7

These perfectly portable paperbacks include the melodies, lyri chords symbols for your favorite songs, all in a convenient, pock book. Using concise, one-line music notation, anyone from hobby professionals can strum on the guitar, play melodies on the piano, c the lyrics to great songs. Books also include a helpful guitar chord ch

'80s & '90s ROCK
00240126

THE BEATLES
00702008

THE BLUES
00702014

CHORDS FOR KEYBOARD & GUITAR
00702009

CLASSIC ROCK
00310058

COUNTRY HITS
00702013

NEIL DIAMOND
00702012

HYMNS
00240103

INTERNATIONAL FOLKSONGS
00240104

JAZZ STANDARDS
00240114

MOTOWN HITS
00240125

MOVIE MUSIC
00240113

ELVIS PRESLEY
00240102

THE ROCK & ROLL COLLECTION
00702020

FOR MORE INFORMATION, SEE YOUR LOCAL MUSIC DEALER,
OR WRITE TO:

7777 W. BLUEMOUND RD. P.O. BOX 13819 MILWAUKEE, WI 53213

Prices, availability and contents subject to change without notice.
Some products may not be available outside the U.S.A.